SIGNOR DOTTORE

By F. MICHELE DANIELE, M.D.

Rime Vecchie e Nuove (New and Old Rhymes)
Calvario de Guerra (Diary of Prison Life)
Yankee Faith and Other Stories
Signor Dottore

Signor Dottore

The Autobiography of
F. Michele Daniele

ITALIAN IMMIGRANT DOCTOR

(1879–1957)

EDITED BY VICTOR ROSEN

EXPOSITION PRESS

New York

EXPOSITION PRESS INC., 386 Fourth Avenue, New York 16, N.Y.

FIRST EDITION

To ITALO
and the memory of
JOSEPH *and* MINNIE
my beloved children

Preface

Afoot and light-hearted I take to the open road,
Healthy, free, the world before me,
The long brown path before me leading wherever I choose.
Henceforth I ask not good-fortune, I myself am good-fortune,
Henceforth I whimper no more, postpone no more, need nothing,
Done with indoor complaints, libraries, querulous criticisms,
Strong and content, I travel the open road.

—WALT WHITMAN

WALT WHITMAN was one of my father's favorite poets.

Near the end of his long and fruitful life, and near the conclusion of these memoirs, my father wrote: "Judged simply and
solely by the worldly measure of things, my life, I am afraid,
could not be called a success story.

"I have not accumulated great wealth; I have not achieved
fame. There are no medical institutions that bear my name. . . .
Thus, from a purely mundane standpoint, my life has been anything but a resounding, resplendent triumph."

Shortly after typing those words, my father passed away. To
me his life was a great success, for he played the roles of husband, father and physician with tenderness, understanding and
great proficiency.

Although we, his children, never knew him too well until

we were adults, his way of life, even at a distance, influenced us tremendously.

I hope his story will be an inspiration to other newcomers to these shores and to young doctors and men of good will everywhere.

I. W. DANIELE

Contents

SIGNOR DOTTORE

PART ONE

1 : I Learn a Motto

PEOPLE CHOOSE CAREERS for many reasons. Some have a natural bent for music, finance or engineering. Myriads are driven by a lust for fame, or by need or greed for money. Others merely follow in their father's furrow or drift into some field of endeavor. A few experience a "call" to dedicate themselves to a great lifework. In my case, hero-worship decided my profession.

My childish adoration and admiration for my maternal uncle, Dr. Giuseppantonio Gamberale, aroused in me an unusual interest in medicine. Although he was not quite such an imposing figure as our family physician, Dr. di Cosenza, he was still reckoned as one of the most distinguished men in the community and was one of the leading physicians in Agnone, where I was born. Naturally he did everything to encourage and foster my infantile interest in the medical profession, and whenever he would visit our house he would spread his broad hands over my head in a kind of priestlike gesture and say to my mother, "This one, he must be a doctor." Unfortunately, he was not able to do more than inspire me, for he died before I was seven. But my mother had shared his sentiments wholeheartedly and with his sudden, untimely death she became determined to dedicate my life and career to continuing his.

This took a great deal of determination, for my father had set his heart on my becoming an engineer. He was a mathematician of no small ability and had taught the subject for a period in the local schools. But as time went on, and I revealed an appalling ineptitude for mathematics, my mother revealed a rock-like resolve to have me follow in my uncle's footsteps. My father relinquished his dream, and by the time I was twelve it was an accepted fact that I would study medicine and become a doctor. My heart filled with joy not only because it was a great tribute to my uncle and what I wanted very dearly, but even more because it represented my first great moral victory in life.

My family was an ancient one in an ancient community. Agnone was the principal industrial city of the province of Molise which is located just above the "spur" of the Italian "boot," on the Adriatic, or eastern, side of central Italy, the Apennines separating it from the province of Lazio, in which is situated the city of Rome. Sprawled along the gentle slope of a plateau, it looks down upon a lush, green valley watered by the winding Verrino River, a branch of the Trigno that empties into the Adriatic. Fifteen miles to the north and roughly parallel to the Trigno flows the Sangro River, where in World War II was fought one of the bloodiest battles in the entire history of the peninsula. But during the last two decades of the 19th century, when I was a boy and growing up, those river valleys were peaceful and fertile, filled with vineyards, olive groves, orchards and carefully cultivated fields. The thought, the threat of war was remote.

The history of that section of Italy is a proud and long one, extending back a good 2,500 years or more to the very earliest dawn of Roman grandeur. It was populated, particularly the province of Molise, by a tribe known as the Samnites. A fierce and hardy race of mountain fighters, they fought and very nearly defeated the Romans in a series of three wars between 343 and 290 B.C. At the battle of the Caudine Forks in 321 B.C. the Roman legions were soundly thrashed, and in order to save the remnants of its army Rome was forced to beg for peace on humiliating terms. The Samnites were such formidable foes, however, that even when the Romans finally succeeded in conquering

them in the Third Samnite War, chiefly by isolating them from
their allies, Rome extended an honorable peace to them, wisely
preferring to keep them as friends and military partners rather
than as slaves.

Anagnia, as Agnone was called in Roman times, was supposed
to have been founded by Samnites fleeing from Aquilonia, about
eight miles southeast of Agnone, when that city was captured
and sacked by the Romans in 293 B.C. When the Greek king
Pyrrhus attacked Rome immediately after the close of the last
Samnite War and invaded the peninsula, Anagnia marked the
point of his furthest advance on Rome in 279 B.C.

Although the descendants of the ancient Samnites have lost
much of their ancestors' belligerence, they have managed to re-
tain many of their outstanding qualities, characteristics and ideals.
Integrity, loyalty, discipline and a strong sense of duty are to this
day traits that are cherished by Molisans. They possess a profound
love of justice and an austere, almost Spartan attitude toward
life. Not for them the *dolce far niente* philosophy that is preva-
lent in much of Italy, especially in the South. Hard work, devotion and seriousness are the foundation stones of the edifice they
have erected for themselves.

My father, who was named Giuseppe, was a striking example
of the spirit of the region. His family was one of the oldest, most
distinguished in Agnone and that section of Italy. He was extremely tall—that being a characteristic of the Daniele as far
back as anyone could remember. His father was named Romolo,
or Romulus, but was generally known as Romoldone, or Big
Romulus; and his fellow townsmen used to say he was so tall
that when he visited Vesuvius he didn't have to climb to its top
to look down into the crater; all he had to do was stand at its
foot and peer down over its rim—to be sure, in order to do it
he *did* have to stand on tiptoe. Although my father bequeathed
me many of his fine, noble qualities of mind and character, he
unfortunately failed to pass on to me the family inheritance of
height and stature. My eldest sister, Angelina, is the only one
among the three surviving children of the eleven he sired who is

unusually tall, and like most women, she has found it more of a handicap than a help.

The motto inscribed on our family coat of arms was *Lavoro e Lealtà*—Labor and Loyalty—and as is not always the case in many families, we were brought up to believe in and live up to it. Over and over again my father would tell me, "If you wish to succeed and achieve a good life, you must work and be honest, not only with others but most of all with yourself."

Even as I write this I can still see him and hear him as he uttered those words, his dark, deep-set eyes glowing with an almost holy light, his deep voice low, throbbing, intense with passion and conviction. His was not a relaxed, tolerant, perhaps too indiscriminate attitude which we so much value today. Most of us would find his standards and code a bit too severe and rigid, and maybe they were. But they possessed many compensating qualities which I believe we could profitably use in this age of juvenile delinquency, lawlessness, violence and social irresponsibility. My father taught his children self-reliance, self-restraint, independence of mind and spirit and, above all, to love and respect justice. It was a somewhat Spartan discipline, but it was invariably kindly and just.

I do not mean to suggest that we ever lacked for affection or understanding from either of our parents. On the contrary, they gave us the deepest, most intense and beautiful kind of love any child can possibly have. It did not take the form of showy, shallow demonstrativeness. Almost from the day I first was able to talk, my father spoke to me as if I were an adult and treated me accordingly, instilling in me at a very early age a sense of responsibility and an awareness of my relationship as an individual to society as a whole. My mother shared this point of view, and though she loved us dearly, she avoided displaying her feelings by indulging in excessive kissing and hugging. "Children should be caressed," she always said, "only when they are asleep."

This may sound strange to modern ears. Psychologists and sociologists are constantly telling us nowadays that juvenile delinquents, homosexuals and other so-called "misfits" are the product of lack of parental affection during childhood and adolescence. Perhaps they are right, but sometimes I wonder.

In my own case, I know there never was a day when I felt neglected, unwanted or misunderstood by my parents. On the contrary, I had the most profound love and respect for them, particularly for my father, whom I regarded as a great man, as a kind, a sympathetic and, above all, a supremely just man. His keen sense of justice was his outstanding quality, the one that shaped and guided his entire existence.

Once, when he was a boy, a gypsy with a dancing bear came to town. My father was in the crowd waiting to see the animal perform. But on that occasion the bear did not perform; perhaps he got temperamental or wasn't feeling well that day. Anyhow, whatever the reason, his trainer got the idea that my father had done something to distract the bear and cause him not to dance, and he gave the boy a whack that knocked him to the ground.

Years passed, and one day the same gypsy returned to Agnone with another trained bear. My father recognized the fellow instantly. He marched straight up to him and flattened him with two mighty blows. "The first punch is in return for the one you gave me when I was a boy," he told him "and the second is eleven years' compound interest."

Father loved to tell that story, not only because it was amusing but, more important, because it served to illustrate what was the most deeply rooted article of his faith: that in this life nothing goes unrewarded or unpunished.

He was not a wealthy man, but he was by no means a poor one either; and besides the roomy, comfortable house we lived in and in which I was born December 28, 1879, he owned a fair amount of property both in the town itself and in the surrounding countryside, including a large farm and a number of vineyards. He operated the farm by sharecropping, furnishing the tenant-farmer the land, tools and seed in return for his labor and one-half of the crops. We virtually lived off our own land, for most of the meat and all the vegetables, fruits and flour we used were raised on it. The clothes we wore were made out of wool that came from the sheep grazing on our pastures and was carded and spun by our own womenfolk. The shoes we walked in were manufactured from the hides of our cattle by one of the local cobblers. This was a somewhat primitive economic system, I grant, but it provided us with food and clothing that was invariably of the finest quality, even though it may not have been the most fashionable. Moreover, it helped to bring home to me yet another of my father's deepest principles: the virtue of self-reliance and independence. I don't believe there has ever been a period in my life since then when I have felt such a complete and profound sense of security as I did during those first two decades of my existence.

Our house in town could not be called "a show place." Except for the fact that it was larger than most, it resembled other structures in Agnone and, for that matter, in most other smaller communities in central and southern Italy. It was of two stories in the rear and three in the front, because of the fact that it was built on a hillside. It was of whitewashed stone, unornamented by any architectural embellishments, solid, spacious and truly as "functional" as the most modern skyscraper. Here my father had been born and had lived his entire life, and his father before him, and his father before him. All told, not including me, some seven or eight generations of my family had dwelled within its walls. Above the massive, severely plain oaken double door that opened onto the Piazza Roma, the principal square of the city, was the only thing that might be regarded as ornamentation—a fierce, snarling lion with an upraised paw resting on a shield upon which was carved the letter D, representing our family name and alluding to our biblical patronym, the Hebrew prophet who succeeded in outstaring the lions.

Although this door was the official and quite impressive entrance to the Palazzo Daniele, as our unpretentious *casa* was generally called, the residence proper—that is to say, our actual living quarters—was located on the second floor. The ground floor served only as a storeroom in which were kept an entire year's supply of wheat, corn, potatoes, fruits and vegetables grown on the family farm. From the beamed ceiling hung massive bunches of grapes, wrapped in paper, and bright garlands of apples, peaches and pears strung together. Braids of garlic, chili peppers and onions were strung on hooks along the walls. The open shelves sagged beneath the weight of huge smoked hams, salamis, sausages and flitches of bacon, enormous cheeses, jars of olive oil, vinegar, lard, tomato paste. In one corner stood barrels of cucumber in brine; in the other, cords of wood and piles of charcoal. Beneath the storeroom, carved out of the solid rock of the hillside, was the wine cellar, filled with row on row of bottled Marsala, muscatel, Chianti, Lagrima Cristi, *Asti spumante* and the finest French and German vintages, for my father loved and knew good wines.

On what was the second, but actually the first, or main, floor was the *salone* or parlor, the library, the *sala da pranzo,* or dining room, and the kitchen, which was dominated by a monstrous fireplace that was wide and deep enough to have held a grand piano comfortably. All the cooking was done in the fireplace, either in kettles or on grills over the open fire. One whole wall of the kitchen was covered with various cooking utensils, all of them, as in every other kitchen in Agnone, made of the purest hammered copper. Since medieval times Agnone had been famed throughout Italy for the excellence and beauty of its copperware, particularly for its church bells, which were produced at a foundry that had been for centuries under the direct patronage of the Vatican and the bells of which were therefore privileged to bear the papal arms. The kitchen also housed another useful apparatus made of copper—a large bathtub, for it was here, in the kitchen, that we did our bathing. What it may have lacked in privacy it more than made up in warmth and comfort. In back of the kitchen was the garden, which contained a small vegetable plot, flower beds and a number of almond, fig and peach trees in addition to a chicken coop, a dovecote and a rabbit hutch. On the top floor of the house were three bedrooms.

It certainly could not be called an elegant establishment, but it was comfortable, cheerful and admirably equipped to fill all our needs and wants. It was, in short, truly a "home" in every sense of the word.

In many respects our *casa* was representative of the general pattern of life in Agnone and perhaps a large part of Italy at that time—simple, inelegant, even a trifle primitive and crude, but supremely pleasant, practical and peaceful. Not that it was without its cares, troubles and struggles. There were quarrels. There were bitter rivalries. There were defeats and disappointments. We had thieves and crooks and drunkards and even an occasional murderer. I can remember, when I was a boy, the entire town being in a state of terror for months because of a gang of burglars who were breaking into houses at night. It wasn't until one of them made the mistake of drinking just a little too much wine and getting *umbriaco* that the police were able to put an end to this "crime wave." And there was the town bully, who made life miserable for all of us kids until our parents solved *that* problem by taking up a collection for him and sending him to South America.

I am quite sure that we must have been just as disturbed and unhappy because of such things as we are today by the cares and misfortunes that assail us constantly. Yet somehow it seems as if life was more relaxed, more serene and more evenly balanced at that time. Put it down, if you like, as the rambling of a senile sentimentalist dreaming of the Good Old Days that perhaps never were. In any case, whether true or not, the fact remains that life in Agnone, and in Italy generally, during that last quarter of the 19th century possessed a serene charm and dignity it has never known since. Why, even going to school was fun. Well, at least relatively speaking.

When I had finished my three years at the Ginnasio Inferiore I was sent to Lucera, about ten miles northwest of Foggia and one of the most ancient towns in Italy, to attend the Ginnasio Inferiore Liceo, which in Italy roughly corresponds to college in the United States. Lucera's history, like Agnone's, dates back to pre-

Roman times. It had figured in the Samnite Wars as an ally of Rome. In A.D. 663 it was destroyed by fire by Constans II, Emperor of the East and was not restored until nearly six centuries later, in 1223, by the Holy Roman Emperor Frederick II, who had some 20,000 Arab slaves brought there to carry out the project. Frederick also erected one of the largest and strongest medieval fortresses there and held his court there in truly oriental magnificence, his impregnable castle containing within its massive walls not only a palace and an arsensal but the emperor's harem, treasury, mint and even a menagerie filled with wild animals. Its battlements and dungeons still dominate the Foggia Plain today as they did 750 years ago.

But it was not because of Lucera's historic significance that I was sent there to complete my preliminary academic education. Another of my mother's brothers, Luigi Gamberale, presided over the Ginnasio Liceo there and was considered one of the leading educators in Italy at that time. He was a famous Latinist, the author of numerous textbooks and the translator of many important German, English and American poets. His Italian renderings of Walt Whitman were particularly admired by literary men and scholars. One of my most prized possessions is a presentation copy of his translation of *Leaves of Grass,* which he inscribed, "To my nephew—this copy in Italian of the poems of the world's greatest modern poet."

But my Uncle Luigi, like my father and so many Italian men of his generation, was of the antique Roman stamp—austere, strong-willed and strict. This applied especially to his students, and he refused to make the slightest concession to the normal high spirits of youth. He was an almost Prussian disciplinarian, and he was particularly severe with me, in order to avoid any hint of favoritism.

My stay at Lucera was terminated the next year, for my uncle was transferred to the Liceo at Campobasso, the capital and largest city of the province of Molise, and much closer to my home. I was accordingly also transferred to Campobasso. The journey from Agnone, not quite twenty-five miles away, took half a day of traveling by train and stagecoach in 1895.

I was sixteen then, and I remained at Campobasso until April, 1899, when a great tragedy befell me and profoundly altered the entire course of my life. I was to receive my baccalaureate degree in June, but two months before that I received word that my father, who had been ill for about a year, had died. My mother had also been ailing for a long time, and now that she was alone she found that maintaining our rather large establishment and supervising its operation was far too much as a physical as well as a financial burden. She sold our house in Agnone, and went to live with my younger sister, Patrizia. At the time of my father's death Patrizia and her husband were living in Canosa, a town far to the south of Agnone, located midway between Foggia and Bari.

Although I had been physically separated from my family during the past eight or nine years while I was going to school, yet spiritually, you might say, there had been no cleavage. At Christmas and Easter, and during the summer holiday I had always returned to the family hearth. No matter for how long or how distantly I might be removed from home, I still felt I had roots, that I belonged, that I had a haven to which I could always return. Now that was suddenly snatched from me, and for the first time in my life I felt naked and alone, cut adrift from all my moorings.

This emotional and psychological loss was further complicated by a critical economic problem. Though we had been fairly well-to-do, like many families whose worldly goods consist principally of real estate we were "land poor," and when my father died there was comparatively little in the way of liquid assets in his estate. Moreover, my sisters had been married only a few years before; that meant that a good part of his cash had been consumed in fulfilling that age-old European custom, the *dote,* or dowries, that had to be paid to his two new sons-in-law. Fortunately, however, he had left me some bonds, and my mother generously gave me a half share of the money she received from the sale of our house in Agnone. This scarcely added up to a fortune, but by dint of prudent management and stringent economizing I was able to spend six years studying medicine at the University of Naples, then considered Italy's foremost medical school.

Five years of a new century were to pass before I was to realize the first tangible result of my hard work and self-denial. Many, many times during that long, bitter period I was almost on the point of turning back in despair and defeat. How many times I asked myself, "Is being a doctor really worth this enormous sacrifice, this heartbreak and sweat?" I don't think I was ever able to answer that question with actual words or thoughts, and if my very life had depended on it, I could not have said why I felt and knew it was worth it. But something deep inside me told me that no amount of toil and struggle and hardship would be too much to pay for the privilege of pursuing my chosen profession. No matter how often or how strongly my purely intellectual processes nudged me and raised doubts as to the practical wisdom of my course, some powerful, mysterious instinct within the profoundest reaches of my being kept driving me on until, at long, long last, I reached that glorious July day in 1905 when I stepped onto the stage of the *teatro* of the University of Naples and received my precious degree of Doctor of Medicine.

I know that thousands, perhaps millions, of men before me and after me have enjoyed that same experience; yet I am certain that for each of them, as for me, it was *the* great moment of their lives, the one that gave them the supreme thrill and the deepest, most soul-satisfying sense of accomplishment and fulfillment. Even today, half a century later, I can still feel all over again the tingling sensation I felt that sunny summer's afternoon as the rector shook my hand, congratulated me and presented me with that paltry yet, oh, so priceless piece of parchment that was my passport into a world I had so long and so ardently coveted.

Nor can I ever forget the thrill of elation I got when, soon afterward, I had occasion to write my name and after it placed those two magic letters—M.D. But actually, what gave me the profoundest joy was that moment when, having received my diploma, I returned to my seat beside my mother and saw the look in her eyes.

It is one thing to say you want to be a doctor and to become one: it is another after you have finally won the right to call yourself one. First of all, a just-hatched physician must decide whether he wants to enter a specialty eventually or to remain in so-called general practice. Today, of course, most young doctors starting out on their careers want to specialize, because that is generally more lucrative and carries more prestige. But in 1905, the Age of Specialization was still in its infancy and many physicians were quite content to remain general practitioners. If I decided to enter some specialty, the next question I would have to answer was what branch of medicine I should go into.

But that was only part of the problem. The fledgling physician, especially in Europe, had also to determine whether he wanted to risk the uncertainties of private practice in the hope of gaining later substantial rewards, or whether he preferred the security of a salaried position with some government agency or some large company, such as a ship's doctor or a factory medical director. Each had its compensations, as well as its disadvantages, and they had to be weighed carefully.

Nor was this all of the doctor's dilemma. Besides determining how he desired to practice medicine, he also had to determine *where* he wanted to practice it.

Like many of my colleagues in Italy in that era, I was faced by still another question. Was it wiser to remain in my own country or to migrate to some other, the United States or one in South America? For in 1905 there were no barriers to immigration. Again, I had to balance the greater security of staying at home, among my own people, against the opportunities offered by boldly adventuring into a new land and attempting to build a practice among strangers.

These, then, were the choices I had to make during that summer of 1905 before I could actually put my as yet small store of knowledge and skill to work for my fellow men and myself. But before I could make that choice there was another I had to make—one that was, in some respects, even more vital to me and that concerned me even more deeply.

2 : *Love Rears Its Lovely Head*

ELVIRA AND I had known each other since we were children in school, but it wasn't until I came back to Agnone during the summer after my first year at medical school that I became really aware of her existence. She was three years younger than I; that explains why, when we were growing up together in Agnone, I never paid any attention to her. To a teen-age boy, a girl three years his junior is a mere baby. To a twenty-year-old youth, however, it is a very different thing, especially if the girl happens to have enormous black eyes, luxuriant black hair, dimpled cheeks, skin like creamy white velvet and an enchanting smile.

Elvira was the daughter of Giovanni Ionata, who was an attorney and the mayor of Agnone. Her family, like mine, was an old one and distinguished. We renewed our acquaintance soon after my return in a quite conventional fashion. Her parents invited me to dinner, and my first infatuation seized me, unromantically enough, over a plate of delicious minestrone. I say "delicious," though actually I had no idea whether it was or wasn't, because I could not taste it at all. I was too busy admiring Elvira to notice anything—except, perhaps, that she appeared to return my interest. Not openly, to be sure; such a thing would be unthinkable for any nice, well-brought-up girl to do. But when I left the Casa Ionata that evening I was sure of two things: one that I loved her; two, that she loved me.

In America, the next move would have been simple and obvious. I would have promptly made a date with her, taken her to a show and then for a snack or a soda; then we would have "kept company" for a while and then announced our engagement. But in Italy—especially in southern Italy—the social conventions are much more rigid and strict. If a boy and girl are seen walking along the street together alone, that means but one thing—the girl's name is blasted forever. Everyone will immediately brand her a tramp and a trollop. Whenever I came to see Elvira the inevitable duenna was present to let the world know that Elvira was a respectable girl and to act as a kind of bouncer in case I might try to get "fresh." Even if we merely wished to take a stroll in broad daylight, her chaperone marched behind us like a bodyguard or a detective.

I think I spent most of that summer vacation hovering about Elvira's house, waiting for her to come out so that I could follow her and maybe exchange a word or just to catch a glimpse of her through a window and wave to her or, if I was sure nobody was around to see me, to blow a kiss at her. When she would go to church, I would be right behind her, concealed by one of the pillars of San Antonio, and if we were lucky and her duenna drowsy, I'd be able to whisper a few words to her. Those three months in Agnone were unquestionably the most religious of my entire existence; never before nor since have I attended church so often.

Occasionally, also, we'd meet in shops or on the street, and I'd greet her ceremoniously, as though we were hardly more than strangers. We would also "happen" to run into each other at parties. At such social events we would always observe the strictest formality, our conversation of the chastest, most conventional character, our behavior impersonal and polite. That is, except while we were dancing or if we could manage to steal a few minutes alone, unobserved, outside in the garden or in some quiet, lonely corner.

Our happiest and most frequent opportunities, however, came late at night. I would wait till the Ionata *casa* was still and dark.

Then I would tiptoe to Elvira's window and, in the best romantic tradition, toss a pebble against it; she would softly open
it, and we would stand there for hours, murmuring all those
sweet platitudes that lovers have been saying to each other ever
since Adam and Eve.

Of course, all these elaborate subterfuges and precautions
were an utterly needless complication (at least, from *our* view-
point), and I heartily cursed them, the antiquated customs of my
country and Elvira's parents for insisting on observing them.

My lot was made a trifle easier, though, when Elvira went
to visit her aunt, Signora Cremonese who owned a large *tenuta,*
or farm estate in the neighboring countryside. There I was able
to bribe one of the maids who was supposed to act as Elvira's
duenna during her visit. The girl, in return for the rather generous sum I gave her, acted as our post office, delivering our
letters for us, as well as standing guard during our many meetings, which took place in a remote spot in the woods.

When I went back to the university in the autumn Elvira
wrote to me two or three times a week and I would answer just
as faithfully, staying up all hours of the night in order to write
her grotesquely long and grotesquely honeyed letters after completing a hard day's studying. Thank heaven the tender passion
afflicts us only when we are young, else our constitutions would
never be able to stand the punishment.

We could have avoided much of this toil and tribulation by
becoming *fidanzata* early in the game. But we wanted to be
absolutely sure we were "right" for each other before becoming
engaged, and until we did so, Italian custom and tradition pro-
hibited us from keeping company. Finally, however, we decided
we wanted to get married, and obtaining the blessings of our
respective families, we announced our betrothal. Since I still had
to complete my medical education, however, we agreed to postpone the wedding until after I graduated from the university.

Thus July, 1905, found me entering two new worlds—that
of medicine, and matrimony. Elvira and I were married in
Agnone, the ceremony solemnized in the Church of San Antonio,

where her family had worshipped for generations and where I had wooed her from behind a pillar, like Mephistopheles in *Faust*.

As I look back on it now, I cannot help marveling a bit at my own boldness (or was it folly?) in taking on the responsibility of a wife and, being young, healthy Italians, the inevitable *bambini* even before I had got launched on my professional career. For now, once the raptures of the honeymoon had begun to fade, I discovered the doctor's dilemma was double. Not only did I have to determine how and where I wanted to practice medicine; I had to make my decision in the light of having a wife and future family to support. In making my choice, I would have to consider not only the all-important factor of income but also how immediately I would be earning money to pay the rent, groceries and clothes and meet other expenses of married life. Thus I could not consult my own wishes alone. I must also consider Elvira and the family that was sure to follow. My course appeared to be clearly indicated: I must seek her advice and views. This I did, and throughout the rest of our life together this was our fixed policy; we never undertook anything that involved us or our children without first talking it over together and arriving at a decision that was agreeable to both of us. In passing, let me add that I would unreservedly prescribe this method of solving family questions to all newly wedded couples —and long-wedded ones, as well.

Had I been in a position to do so, I would have gone on with my studies, specialized in dermatology and eventually gone on to teach. But that would have required two things, neither of which I possessed in any great quantity: one, money; two, time. My only alternative, then, was to go into practice immediately as a general practitioner.

Since hanging out my shingle would call for a rather sizable outlay in order to provide furniture, instruments and all the other incidentals that go with setting up an office, especially in any larger community, I seriously considered taking an institutional position, either as staff physician with one of the bigger indus-

trial concerns in Milan, Turin or one of the other northern cities
or as ship's doctor with one of the steamship lines. All of these
would have guaranted me an immediate and steady income.

Elvira and I weighed each of them very carefully. I pointed
out the plus and minus features in each, trying to be as objective
as I could. On one hand, it meant giving up one's independence
and submitting to some form of institutional discipline and dic-
tation. On the other, I would only be able to see Elvira in between voyages.

That, then, reduced the area of choice to going into private
practice and not specializing. The only thing left to be decided
was where to set up shop. Should I remain in Italy, and if so,
should I practice in Agnone, where I was known but where
there were already more physicians than were needed? Or should
I go to one of the big cities—Naples, Rome, Venice, Milan? Or
to one of the smaller rural communities?

By 1905, Italy had managed to get a feeble paw into the
imperialist grab bag and had acquired a few sand-strewn colonies
in Africa, and my fellow countrymen were constantly being persuaded, nudged and prodded into emigrating in order to relieve
the pressure of overpopulation at home that was threatening to
burst the Italian "boot" at the seams. The government particularly encouraged young doctors to settle in our colonial possessions, but I had little taste for living among savages in a sun-
parched wilderness or in steaming jungles. Moreover, I had no
intention of subjecting the woman I loved and the children I
hoped and expected to have to such living conditions. Much as I
like adventure, I drew the line at some places, and Africa was
one of them.

Unless I wanted to stay in Italy, then, my only other alternative was to migrate to the Argentine, Brazil or the United
States. The South American countries would, of course, be much
less difficult to tackle, since the language problem would be much
simplified and culturally they were much closer to Italy than
the United States was. But by the same token, the opportunities
were far greater to the north "where the streets were paved with

gold." And since my whole purpose in emigrating was to seek just precisely that—opportunity—it seemed as if my most practical course was to head for the United States.

Convincing Elvira's family and mine, however, was quite another matter. At that time, only the lowest, poorest, most illiterate element of Italy's population emigrated—what my father-in-law scornfully called the *canaglia,* the rabble. Why should a supposedly sane, intelligent, educated man want to give up his comforts, his security and position, to seek his fortune among strangers who, according to some of the stories that drifted back, looked upon foreigners, and especially Italians, with contempt or even outright hatred?

Papa Ionata was also opposed to it because it was a kind of reflection on him. After all, he was mayor of Agnone. He commanded considerable power and influence in that part of the world, and it was to be expected that he would be able to do much to advance the career of his new son-in-law. Most young men, he told me, would willingly sell their souls to the devil in order to obtain such backing. Instead of which, here I was spurning his assistance and dragging his beloved daughter off to a wilderness, to live among barbarians. What would people say? What would they think? They might get the impression that his own son-in-law had no faith in his influence and political strength. Thanks to my crazy ideas, he, Giovanni Ionata, *sindaco* and first citizen of Agnone, was likely to be ruined himself. I ought to be locked up in a lunatic asylum.

But Elvira joined her pleas with mine and backed up my arguments with surprising passion and conviction, and finally we succeeded in persuading him not to oppose our plans. Grudgingly he and the other members of our families yielded, bowing before the inevitable. They gave us their blessings and wished us Godspeed, and on November 21, 1905, we sailed from Naples aboard the White Star liner *Cretic* for the United States.

The greatest adventure of my life had begun.

3 : America Is Discovered Again

No ONE WHO HAS NOT HAD the experience of emigrating to a strange, new land can possibly know and understand what it is like. Any transplantation must always be a painful, difficult operation. I am trying to recall my own feelings as objectively as possible. I approached the shores of my adopted land with great excitement, it is true, but not with any sense of elation or gladness. If I were to analyze my mood during those first days of December, as the *Cretic* drew nearer New York, I would say it was compounded rather of fear, of doubt, of sadness and of regret and aching nostalgia. And I must confess that my first glimpse of the Statue of Liberty on the morning of December 5 did not send a thrill of delight and anticipation through me. On the contrary, it only served to remind me of all that I had left behind—my family, my friends, my home. Perhaps if my background had been somewhat humbler or my economic status less secure, I might have been more excited by that symbol of freedom and opportunity. Yet I honestly doubt that even the poorest, lowliest *paesano* experienced any different sensation than I did as I leaned against the ship's rail and gazed up at the serene goddess outlined against the gray wintry sky. This, I fully appreciate, shatters one of the dearest stereotypes of romantic legend, cherished by sentimental novelists, playwrights and moviemakers for half a century or more.

Nor was my nervous apprehension in any degree lessened by my first contact with the people among whom I had chosen to live. We were herded onto Ellis Island and examined, questioned and microscopically scrutinized before being permitted to set foot upon American soil. Of course I should have recognized the fact that bureaucracy is the same the world over, and that our own Italian petty officialdom was just as offensive. It took us endless hours to run the gantlet of customs, immigration and health authorities; several times during the course of that minor inquisition I was on the point of exploding, but luckily Elvira was always able to sense it and to check it by a glance, a smile, a tug at my arm or a gently whispered word or two—*Un po' di pazienza, carino mio:* "A little patience, my love."

But all things human must end, even the worst, and we were finally turned loose and put upon a small boat that would take us across the choppy, garbage-laden waters of New York Bay to Manhattan and its pavements of solid gold.

Just as the ferry began to pull away from the dock I saw the spectacle of the mighty metropolis suddenly rising up from its watery bed. The heaven-challenging rampart of skyscrapers that girds Manhattan Island today was only beginning to take shape then; but already one or two of the monstrous *gratticieli,* as we called them in Italy, had reared up to unbelievable heights of four and five hundred feet; and to one who came from a country where a four-story building was considered tall, a structure that was ten or twelve stories high was utterly overwhelming. That first glimpse of New York stunned, and dazzled, and bewildered me. It seemed totally unreal, and during that entire trip across the bay I kept telling myself that I was awake, that this was not some incredible vision out of Dante's *Paradiso,* an incantation that would vanish as abruptly as it came.

But this was definitely a case of distance lending enchantment. Once the boat had landed us at the Battery and we disembarked and started uptown to our hotel, our impression of New York had to be radically revised. No longer was it something out of the *Paradiso* but, rather, out of the *Inferno.* Never in my life had

I found myself plunged into such a frenzied maelstrom of carriages, cabs, primitive autos and enormous trucks drawn by horses as big as elephants and driven by giants who looked as if they had stepped right out of the Wagnerian operas. Even in that long, long ago—in that era which we now look back on so wistfully as a period of restful quiet, peace and leisurely contentment—even then there was a "traffic problem" in New York.

In and around and among that frantic tide of wheeled traffic surged a churning stream of human traffic, rushing, trotting, scurrying, plunging in between, alongside and sometimes (so it seemed) even under and above the vehicles.

And the noise! Above the constant grumble of the wagons, autos, drays and carriages could be heard the banging of the horsecars, the clanging of their bells and the clickety clatter of the el trains racing overhead—an utterly startling and improbable sight, railroad trains suspended in midair! And mingling with this incessant symphony of noise, forming a kind of steady counterpoint, was the sound of human voices talking, laughing, shouting, cursing, whispering.

It was indeed a strange, wondrous new world we had come to, and not a little frightening. In Italy, emigrants returning from the United States had always extolled the beauties and splendors of New York, "the greatest city in the world," and it came as quite a shock and a letdown to find that its streets were narrow, crowded, dirty and unimpressive, that its citizens were quite ordinary-looking, anything but the smartly-dressed, well-groomed paragons of worldly style I had pictured. Their bizarre customs and ways, however, surprised and puzzled me the most. For one thing, they never stopped rushing about. Where they were rushing to or why was something I could not comprehend—and, for that matter, still cannot. And all of them seemed angry about something. Or if not angry, at least worried. In the throngs I saw along Broadway and Fifth Avenue I could not detect a single happy, carefree face.

I had carefully prepared myself for this adventure both by

familiarizing myself with the history and geography of the United States and by studying English. Indeed, I was quite proud of my newly acquired fluency in that strange, somewhat barbaric tongue. Now that I was at last among the people who spoke it, I was eager to show off my skill in front of Elvira.

My first opportunity came the day after our arrival. I had been fascinated by the elevated railroad. Somehow, it seemed to violate all the laws of Nature, especially that of gravity. So right after breakfast Elvira and I set out to take our first excited, albeit somewhat fearful ride on the el. We had no difficulty finding it or the station; it was right down the street from our hotel, as I had carefully observed the night before. We climbed the steep stairs to the platform. Not knowing what the fare was and suddenly finding myself at a loss to recall a single English word, I placed the largest silver coin I had in my pocket in front of the ticket-seller and hoped for the best. It must have been a dollar, for he gave me two tickets and an enormous collection of small coins. Of course I had no idea what we were supposed to do with the tickets, but I noticed other people tossing theirs into an open-topped glass box with a kind of chopping knife inside it that was presided over by a shaggy, bored-looking old man in a dusty, faded blue uniform. I did the same and Elvira and I went past the shabby Cerberus onto the cold, windswept platform.

Up and down, to right and left, as far as the eye could see stretched slim, glistening silver veins. In the distance, perhaps half a mile away or more, we could make out tiny gray bugs moving toward us along the tracks. Presently they began to grow very large, to take shape and form. A muffled rumble could be heard, becoming louder and ever louder, swelling into a deafening roar. We could feel the platform beneath our feet begin to throb, then quiver like a living thing, then sway to and fro like a palm tree in a hurricane. Elvira's face turned white. Her dark eyes widened in terror and her slender fingers bit into my arm. "*Gran Dio!*" she murmured, crossing herself. I tried to reassure her, but I was just as scared as she was. In fact, I was just on the point of grabbing her and rushing back down to the street, but I realized that it was too late; the entire station seemed to be coming apart. I was sure that at any second the platform would collapse and we would all be plunged to our deaths in the street below. I decided the best thing we could do, the only thing we could do, was to cling tightly to each other and die in each other's arms. I seized her in my embrace and she buried her face in my none-too-manly bosom.

By now the noise had become deafening. A moment later the train sped into the station and came to a grinding halt. We had lost all desire to ride on it, but by this time a crowd that had gathered behind us shoved and pushed aboard the cars, carrying us helplessly along with it.

For several minutes after we were on it Elvira and I kept our eyes shut, clutching each other's hands. But when we had traveled some distance and apparently were still safe and unharmed, I tentatively opened one eye and took a quick look around. What I saw was quite astonishing. Our fellow passengers were calmly sitting and standing in the car, many of them reading newspapers, books and magazines, others talking loudly above the clatter of the wheels, some just staring out of the windows. None of them seemed frightened. It scarcely seemed possible that *all* of them should be oblivious to the danger.

It began to dawn on me, then, that maybe there was no danger at all, that for all its shaking and shivering, its roaring and rattling, the el was quite safe. I observed the others more carefully. All of them looked and acted as if riding on these hellish contraptions was a habitual, commonplace experience. Nothing in their behavior indicated the slightest stress or excitement. I pressed Elvira's arm and whispered to her to open her eyes, we had nothing to fear. She raised her lids slowly, suspiciously. She gazed around the car. Apparently what she saw made her feel a little more confident, too, for she looked at me and gave me a pale little smile that told more eloquently than words her child-like embarrassment and still lingering uncertainty.

The train was not too crowded, and we had no trouble finding places side by side on one of the facing seats near the middle of the car. I wanted her to sit by the window, but she was afraid of looking out over the edge of the tracks into the street that seemed to be miles below us. She preferred to sit beside the aisle so she would have less of a feeling of being suspended in the air. (In later years she never overcame her dread of riding on the elevated and invariably refused to travel on it unless I was with her. Even then, she would do so only with extreme reluctance. Naturally I never insisted on it, so I doubt that she ever again set foot on what she called *il treno del diavolo*—the devil's train.)

After I had got used to it, I found myself enjoying the trip. It was a strange, startling sensation, speeding at thirty or forty miles an hour and all the while being able to steal fleeting glimpses into other people's private lives.

There was one point on the line, after we had been traveling for perhaps half an hour, where the tracks soared to an incredible height and then suddenly made a sharp, sweeping, utterly breath-taking curve into what seemed like empty space, with no buildings on either side. I made the mistake of peering down out of the window. The ground must have been hundreds of feet beneath us—or so it seemed—and the people and vehicles moving about looked like insects and toys. I got dizzy. As the train raced around that enormous arc I pictured it in my mind leaving the tracks, sailing out into space and crashing to the pavement below.

I seized Elvira's hand and waited for the first grinding, grating noise that would tell me the dreadful thing had started. But the only sound I could hear was the normal *click-clack* of the wheels, only now somewhat sharper, more distinct and staccato, as I felt the train slowing down. "Ah! Perhaps the engineer has decided to stop," I said to myself, "before disaster overtakes us." I felt the train stop. Then I heard voices and the shuffling of feet. I half opened my eyes. To my surprise I found we were in another station. People were getting off and on quite calmly. Again, we had escaped a catastrophe.

We rode on for another thirty or forty minutes into a region that seemed more sparsely settled. Here I observed many small wooden houses as well as a sprinkling of larger brick ones that were four or five stories high. There were many empty fields, some of them strewn with gigantic boulders and cliffs, and I saw flocks of goats grazing in some of them and even an occasional cow here and there.

Now the car became more and more deserted, and presently Elvira and I were the only ones in it, save for the blue-coated conductor, who would shout some strange, incomprehensible, singsong incantation each time the train began to slow down as it approached a station. But it was very pleasant and cozy, having the car all to ourselves. Outside, the bare fields and streets were blanketed with snow and the people we saw breathed out billowing clouds of steam in the clear, sharp wintry air. But here, inside our private railway carriage, it was snug and warm and peaceful, except when the train gave an occasional abrupt lurch and we thought it was going to pitch off the rails. I clasped Elvira's little hand in mine, and we whispered affectionate nonsense to each other and, when we thought the conductor wasn't looking, stole a kiss.

Again, the train stopped. The conductor slid open the front door of the car, stuck his head in and yelled out something. Then he went out onto the platform.

"*Che dice?*" Elvira asked. "What's he saying?"

I shrugged. "*Non importa,*" I said. "It doesn't matter."

Several minutes passed. Elvira and I were too busy with our love talk to notice. Presently it struck me that the train had stopped at this station for an unusually long time. I wondered why, but then dismissed it from my mind as of no particular consequence.

It began to get cold. The conductor had left the door open. I got up and was going to close it when he reappeared and bellowed out something once more. This time, though, there was a certain impatience and even a hint of anger in his tone. But I had no idea what he was saying. Elvira asked me again what he said, and again, unwilling to admit my ignorance, I said it was nothing important.

But apparently the conductor thought it was. He strode over to me, grabbed my arm and yelled what must have been something like, "All off! End of the line!" Then, seeing we did not understand, he pointed to the platform and then violently gestured to us to get off the train. It took a little while until we understood his pantomime, but finally we got it, though by then he had practically dragged us out of the car himself. When we reached the platform he pointed toward the front end of the train and at long last we were able to realize what he was trying to tell us, for the tracks came to an abrupt end.

But now we found ourselves faced with a real problem. How were we to get back where we came from? To be sure, we could return by the same means by which we had got to this empty wilderness. But what train did we take? Where did we board it? And, most crucial question of all, where did we get off to return to our hotel?

Here was my golden opportunity to display my linguistic skill. Out of the corner of my eye I could see Elvira waiting for me to demonstrate what I could do. Although she loved me very much and was fiercely proud of me, I sensed that she was more than a little doubtful of my vaunted, loudly self-advertised mastery of the English language. As she stood there beside me on that icy platform, her tiny teeth chattering, I could feel her skepticism even more than I could feel the biting cold.

I buckled on my armor and plunged into the battle. Trying to picture in my mind each page of the English dictionary and the grammar I had studied, I painfully and haltingly attempted to ask the conductor how to get back to where we had started. God only knows what it sounded like. In my overweening intellectual pride, I thought I was speaking with the utmost correctness and clearness.

"How . . . do . . . we . . . return——" Now I had to pause, trying to grope for the words I wanted. ". . . whence . . . we . . . issued?"

Even if by some miracle he had been able to understand the words I spoke, I doubt that he would have understood what they meant. He stared at me blankly, his eyes blinking, trying to make up his mind whether I was making fun of him or whether I might really be in earnest. He continued to look at me and scratched the back of his neck. I began to repeat my question for the third time, but suddenly a light came into his gray face and he held up his hand for me to stop. He disappeared inside the station. After a few seconds he returned accompanied by a squat, swarthy man. I took one look at the newcomer and breathed a deep sigh of relief; he was unmistakably Italian or of Italian extraction, I thought; that was why the conductor had fetched him—to act as an interpreter.

The conductor said something to me in English that I did not catch and pointed to the dark-haired fellow. I immediately broke into a grateful flood of Italian, explaining our plight to him and asking for directions. To my amazement, however, the newcomer only stared at me as dumbly as the conductor had done before.

"*Io sono Italiano,*" I said and then added carefully in English, "Me—I——" I jabbed my forefinger against my chest to indicate that I was referring to myself, and they nodded vigorously to indicate they understood that. "Me . . . Ee-ta-lee-an." But that was too much for them, so I repeated very slowly and very emphatically, "Ee-ta-lee-an."

A moment passed. Then the swarthy one's black eyes flashed and he exclaimed, "*Da! Da!* Me—me Polack!" I wasn't sure what "Polack" meant, but it sounded a lot like our word *Polacco,* so I guessed he must be a Pole. In any case, I was now certain he wasn't Italian.

The conductor started speaking in English, and I in Italian and what I thought was English, and the Pole in his weird mixture of grunts and hisses. No one was getting anywhere, and all of us might still be there if it had not been for Elvira and her woman's ingenuity and common sense. She opened up her handbag and pulled out a piece of paper. She showed it to the conductor, pointing to something at the top of it, then pointing to me and herself, then pointing toward the direction we had come and finally pointing again to the paper.

She had to go through this dumb show before he grasped what she meant. He bobbed his head briskly several times and grinned. He took the stump of a pencil out of his pocket and scrawled something on the paper and handed it to Elvira, motioning to us to get back on the train. She looked at me and I looked at her in utter bewilderment. Hadn't he just chased us off it? He apparently realized the cause of our confusion, for he laughed softly, took Elvira's hand and led her back to the very same car we had just left and ushered her aboard it as if she were a queen stepping into the royal private car. Then by means of some of the most strenuous pantomime I have ever witnessed he succeeded in making us understand that when he reached the place he had written on the paper he would personally see to it that we were notified.

We settled down in the same seat we had occupied before and waited for the train to start again. I asked Elvira to show me the mysterious scrap of paper that had proved so much more effective than three languages. It was a piece of blank stationery from our hotel with a picture of the building and the name, address and telephone number printed across the top. On it our conductor friend had written in a wavery scribble: "28 st stashun."

Whoever said one picture is worth a thousand words knew whereof he spoke.

4 : A Greenhorn in "The City of the Young"

WHEN I HAD FIRST DETERMINED to quit Italy and seek a home and a career in America, I had made what nowadays would be called an "informal survey." I realized that my best hope of getting established there lay among my own people. If I could succeed in building a medical practice among other Italian immigrants and winning the reputation I believed my talents, training and hard work could earn for me, then later I might be able to extend my practice to include others beside Italians and those of Italian extraction.

Pursuing this premise to its logical conclusion, I went to considerable pains to learn not only which cities in the United States had the largest percentage of Italian population, but also where there might be the heaviest concentration of former residents of Agnone and the neighboring region. My researches revealed that the American community that contained the largest number of ex-Agnonesi was in a place called La Città dei Giovani, The City of the Young. Although I had no intention of specializing in pediatrics, it still seemed like an auspiciously named place for a young doctor with a young wife seeking to launch a career in a young new world. When I inquired as to its exact location, however, I received nothing but vague answers. I was informed that it was near, or in, or at, or by, or just outside a place called "O-ee-o." For weeks I had pored over geographies, atlases and encyclopedias, trying to find out where in the United States the City of the Young might be situated, but to no avail. I bought gigantic maps of the United States, showing every city, town, village, hamlet, river, lake, pond and puddle, and I combed over them with a magnifying glass methodically, covering them area by area starting in Maine and working south and west. But nowhere could I find a place with such a name. I became as frustrated and infuriated searching for this mysterious city as I had once witnessed in one of the finest surgeons in Italy grappling for a "hot" appendix that had disappeared behind the patient's caecum and stomach. The more I found myself stymied, the more desperate and determined I became to track down that mystery town. After all, there were supposed to be more than two thousand Agnonesi living and working in it, wherever it might be.

I was nearly on the point of giving up in despair when, as such things have a way of doing, my problem was solved almost by itself. One afternoon I dropped into the Café Roma for the customary post-siesta *caffè espresso* and daily exchange of gossip. One of my old school friends, Aldo Campara, beckoned me over to his table and invited me to join him; he had a letter he wanted to read to me.

"Aldo *caro*," I said, "I am not in the mood to listen to love letters, no matter how passionate or spicy——"

"Ah, but this is not a love letter, Michelino!" he said. "This is from my cousin in America, the one who is in the place you wish to go, the City of the Young."

"*Va bene*—okay," I said wearily and sat down at his table with my small cup of fragrant, steaming, tar-black coffee.

Aldo pulled a much-crumpled envelope from his pocket and extracted a letter from it and began reading in a dead, level droning monotone. It was none too intelligibly written to begin with, and his recital did nothing to improve its very limited intelligibility.

My first impulse was to let him mumble on to the end of it. But suddenly something impelled me to reach across the table, snatch the letter out of his hands and exclaim impatiently, "Let me read it for myself. I can get much more out of it with my eyes than my ears." I scanned its contents. There wasn't much in it that I didn't know already. Aldo's *cugino* told about the fantastic amounts he was earning; he was getting paid 125 liras a week, which, in American money, came to $25 a week. In 1905, even in the United States, this was a princely sum. He wrote that he was working in a steel mill, shoveling coal into the big furnaces. But the life in America was *magnifica*. There was plenty to eat and it was good and cheap. And there were plenty of *ragazze* also; maybe some of them were not so young or so good to look at, but for fifty cents you could always have one, and for a dollar you could have one as "beautiful as Cleopatra." His sole complaint about his new home was that he could not get any good *vino*. That is, he could get it, if he was willing to pay for it. A bottle of Italian Chianti cost a quarter, more than a lira! There were lots of American wines and they cost very little, but they weren't worth "washing your feet in." He concluded with a couple of paragraphs about various family matters which, naturally, were of even less interest to me than the rest of his letter.

I folded the sheets of cheap, lined paper and slid them back into the envelope. As I did so my eye happened to fall on the postmark. It said: "Youngstown, Ohio."

It took an instant or two to register. Then suddenly it exploded in my brain.

"Aldo, you say your cousin is in the City of the Young?"

He nodded. *"Si, sì!"*

I looked at the postmark again. My knowledge of English was by then sufficient to tell me that *giovani* means "young" in English, and *città* means "city" or "town." Thus Youngstown, translated very literally, would emerge in Italian as *La Città dei Giovani*—The City of the Young Ones. And as for "Ohio," in Italian it would be written exactly the same, but pronounced as

I had heard it pronounced, "O-ee-o." At long last the tormenting mystery was solved and Mohammed had finally found his Medina.

Before Elvira and I had left Italy, our numerous relatives and friends had alerted their relatives and friends in Youngstown to the fact that two more Agnonesi were headed in that direction, and that not only were we the children of two of Agnone's most distinguished families, but what was of far more consequence, I was one of the most brilliant young physicians in Italy. That I had as yet done almost no actual doctoring was of small matter to our generous, well-intentioned sponsors.

It was no surprise, therefore, to discover that the entire Italian population of Youngstown knew we were arriving on December 8 and were anxiously expecting us. But what *was* a surprise was to find that a reception committee of well over a hundred persons, complete with banners, signs, flags and a brass band, was waiting for us when we descended at the old Pennsylvania Station. After a flowery address of welcome by a house-painter named Umberto Saulino, we were enthroned in an undertaker's carriage and escorted to a large frame house that was sadly in need of repainting. It belonged to none other than Mr. Saulino and his brother Ciro, who was his partner in the house-painting business. Here we were to stay temporarily, until we could find a place of our own.

Elvira and I were exhausted by our trip. Pullmans were a decided novelty to us and that, together with our natural excitement, had kept up from getting much sleep on the train. From the time we arrived until very late that night there was a constant stream of visitors come to greet us, to look us over, to question us about their families and friends in Agnone, to brief us on our new home or to offer us help and advice.

As soon as the discussion would leave the subject of Agnone and Italy, it would turn to the United States and what they thought of it and how they liked it or didn't like it. It seemed to me that in every instance these former Agnonesi either loved their new home with a passionate, even frantic devotion or else detested it with equal fervor and were waiting only until they had amassed enough *soldi Americani* to return to Italy and live like kings for the rest of their lives. Those who had accepted American ways and ideas, however, were fiercely proud of their new allegiance, particularly if they had already obtained United States citizenship or had even taken out first papers. When I would ask these how long they had been in America, they would simply wave their hand and smile and say, "Long, long time! Few months after Cristoforo Colombo come, I come!"

Despite the rather late hour when the festivities finally broke up and lack of sleep the previous night on the train, my curiosity stimulated me so strongly that I got up early next morning and right after breakfast set out to see Youngstown for myself. I have always found that the best way to get acquainted with any city is to prowl about it, at random, in leisurely fashion, looking in shop windows, eating in various restaurants, going into stores, inspecting the public buildings and so on. In that way, by mingling with its people, you get the "feel" of a city better.

Within an hour I had begun to get the "feel" of Youngstown. In 1905 it was still a small place; its population was in the neighborhood of 50,000, perhaps (in 1950 it was 170,000), but it was what Chamber of Commerce boosters like to call "a little big town." There was a feeling of growth, of constantly burgeoning new life, about the community and its people. It never seemed to sleep. There was ceaseless activity seven days and nights a week. At times it irritated me and made me nervous and deeply troubled.

Youngstown was—and still is, of course—primarily a metals-manufacturing center. Even at that time its steel and pig-iron mills were among the largest producers in the United States. The entire town seemed to be fenced in by tall chimneys belching dense clouds of yellow, black, gray and blue smoke as the blast furnaces roared ceaselessly. And at night the clouds hung over the city like a baleful canopy, reflecting the red glare of the furnaces.

I have always preferred the company of a few close friends to running with whole herds of indiscriminate acquaintances.

But I knew when I settled in Youngstown that at least at the start I would have to do a good deal of socializing simply as a matter of professional policy. Not only was it important from the standpoint of making myself known; it would afford me an opportunity to gain some insight into my future patients, how they lived, their background, their attitudes and ideas. Even then, before I had actually started on my career, I had realized that in order to effect cures it is not enough just to treat the disease— the whole man has to be treated as well. And to do that it is essential to know and to understand him as a human being, not merely as a collection of pathological symptoms. Thus all the party-going Elvira and I did during those first weeks in Ohio, besides providing us with much pleasure, served a highly practical purpose. Quietly I would be studying everyone I met, drawing them out in conversation, asking discreet but searching questions about themselves, their children or their families, classifying them and filing away the information in my brain for future reference.

The basic pattern of life among most of the Italians in Youngstown and, for that matter, everywhere else in the United States at that time was pretty much the same. With very few exceptions, they had not yet graduated to the stage of Italo-Americans or the still further advanced stage of being Americans "of Italian extraction," and ultimately just plain, proud, un-hyphenated Americans. In the early 1900's only a scant handful had been in the United States for as long as ten years and the vast majority probably much fewer than five. The slow, painful process of assimilation and adjustment was really only starting. Human beings alter their habits and ways of thinking reluctantly, particularly if their former cultural, economic and social background was narrow and deeply inbred. Most of those first-generation Italian immigrants were, after all, peasants, with all the virtues and the shortcomings of the peasant mentality the world over. Even in Italy they had not been noted for their progressiveness.

I was quite astounded by how much they had changed their

ways already. Many of them had forsworn wine in favor of what might be termed "the wine of the country" of their adoption. They dressed differently, too, though this was more a matter of compulsion than choice, since the only way they could continue to wear clothes *nel modo Italiano* was to have them made to order, and that was expensive. Their houses were utterly unlike anything they had known at home. Here most of them either occupied small wooden one-, two- or three-family dwellings that stood in identical rows or else, in the case of most of the unmarried men, lived in furnished rooms or boarding houses. And of course, the very nature and character of their work here was totally different from anything they had ever known or done in Italy. Here they toiled, stripped to the waist, in front of enormous fiery furnaces or in rolling mills or operated complex machines. Back home they had plowed fields, sowed grain or tended vines or orchards in the sunlight and open air. This was a profound and far-reaching change.

Yet no matter how much they might appear to yield and to accept American methods and manners, their surrender was largely superficial. They still gave everything they did, and wore, and said, and thought that "Italian touch." They managed to give to their undistinguished houses individual accents by planting tiny gardens in the front yards, or by a religious statue or a painting over the door, or some other piece of decoration that would set it apart from all others on the street. Similarly, though they had to wear ready-made American dresses and suits, they succeeded in stamping them with an unmistakable Italian character, even if only by the addition of a colorful bunch of artificial flowers or the wearing of a particularly vivid necktie.

The interiors of their houses remained stubbornly Italian. No matter how American they might appear from the street, once you stepped inside the houses you knew that Italians—and only Italians—could occupy those premises. That they were spotlessly clean, I know, could hardly be considered uniquely an Italian characteristic. But the furniture and the decorations instantly and inescapably marked them as Italian. Much of it, I grant, was tasteless, vulgar and gross. Yet for all its loudness and cheapness, it had the breath of life in it; it was warm, alive and colorful. You could find in every one of them gaudily painted religious images with votive candles in ruby, sapphire, emerald or amber glasses burning beneath them. You could also find in all of them brilliantly tinted large wall calendars, generally depicting some battle or great historic event that took place during Italy's Risorgimento, that resurgence or second Renaissance that resulted in her unification in 1870. You would see the walls strewn with crude, but gaily colored chromos, watercolors and, occasionally, a "genuine, hand-painted" oil painting, their subjects generally either the Madonna or one of the saints, views of Venice and Naples with Vesuvius smoking in the distance (which out-stripped all others), portraits of Garibaldi, Kings Victor Em-manuel II, Umberto I and Victor Emmanuel III, Verdi, Mazzini and Elena, queen to the then Italian ruler—and in that order of popularity. In some few houses, whose occupants were making a more conscious effort to become Americanized, you might find photographs of Teddy Roosevelt, William Jennings Bryan or Ad-miral Dewey.

The furniture especially in the parlor, would almost without a single exception be elephantine in its proportions, usually up-holstered in bright blue, green, crimson or even burnt-orange plush. In the more prosperous homes would be heavy draperies of red, blue or purple gold damask or thick velvet. In many of them you might find an upright piano, particularly if there were youngsters in the family, and in some few there might also be a hand-cranked phonograph with a huge bell-type horn and a stack of Caruso, Scotti, Tettrazini and Bonci records. And this was equally true of Brooklyn, Chicago, Pittsburgh, Boston, San Francisco and everywhere else in the United States where there were "Little Italys."

And just as they clung to their Latin tastes in decorating the interiors of their houses, so they clung to those same Latin tastes when it came to their food. They remained firmly faithful to *la cucina Italiana,* Italian cuisine. As one of my Youngstown friends put it, "There are two things us Wops brought over from the old country we'll never lose—our love of Italian food and our ability to produce *bambini.*" If anyone were to doubt their loyalty to the Italian style of cooking, all he needed to do to convince himself was to walk into any Italian household in Youngstown—or any other American city. There he would find garlands of fragrant salami, spiced sausages, garlic, onions and chili peppers hanging from the kitchen ceiling and sometimes, when there no longer was any space there, also in the bedroom or the parlor.

On the whole, my compatriots seemed quite content with their new life in a new world; but there was one thing almost all of them were unhappy about and resented bitterly. Although an Italian had discovered America and another had given it his name, and still another had claimed North America for England; and although Italians were called on to perform the toughest, most dangerous labor in American industry and had helped to build its railroads, bridges, buildings, highways, churches, schools and hospitals; yet no Italians were being given a voice in the political life of the United States. To the majority of so-called "native" Americans—that meant anyone whose father or mother had been born here—we were all "dirty, ignorant Dagos" or "Wops" and therefore entitled to have no part in public affairs, except maybe to vote, and even then we were expected to sell our vote for a dollar or two to the district boss, whose job it was to deliver the vote in a nice, neat package each November.

We were political outcasts, we had to work extremely hard for whatever we got, our living conditions were not ideal, our health deteriorated. But then, where could one find any kind of existence that did not have its drawbacks and shortcomings?

No; it was quite apparent to any thoughtful man that this great social experiment was going to work out successfully. For all their grumbling, for all their stubborn determination to cling to Italian food, Italian styles, Italian customs and Italian ideas, my fellow expatriates were gradually but inexorably being Americanized, and no matter how much they might complain or resist, they were satisfied with the final result. Even 'way back in 1905 there were manifold evidences that the assimilation process was working successfully. For instance, the younger element among the immigrant population—men and women around my age and Elvira's—were already starting to shed many of their more obviously Italian traits. They were applying themselves diligently to learning English, for one thing, and by the same token speaking Italian as little as possible. They were seeking out American friends and associating with them whenever they could. They cultivated a taste for American dishes and became passionate devotees of that most American of all American institutions, the Chinese restaurant, devouring mountains of chop suey, chow mein and fried rice. They became ardent sports enthusiasts, and as the years went by, the sports pages became studded with more and more Italian names. They went to night schools and studied and slaved to improve themselves. They learned American business, industrial and professional methods. They became naturalized as quickly as they could.

And many of them, either through eagerness to show that they wanted to be good Americans or to escape the stigma of being called Wop or Dago, did not remain content with Americanizing themselves; they also Americanized their names. Sometimes this would produce some grotesque and laughable results. Thus I found that one of my patients named Giovanni Pasta had become transformed into John Dough. Another whose name had been Michele Noci suddenly blossomed forth as Michael Nuts. Our butcher, who had come into the world as Antonio Vacca, now appropriately rechristened himself in the New World, Anthony Cow. Or Vittorio Pizza was translated with grim literalness into Victor Pie and Guglielmo Capra into William Goat— which in its turn soon was popularly translated into Billy Goat.

These name-changings were childish and ridiculous, of course, yet underlying them was a significant fact: they gave indisputable proof that most of the Italian-born newcomers had a deep, sincere love for the country of their choice and genuinely desired to remain in it and to make its future their future. And although I never changed my name to Daniels, not wishing even to imply that I was ashamed of my Italian origin and heritage, I shared that love and desire wholeheartedly. I was glad I had come to America.

5 : I Begin With an Incurable Patient

IT HAPPENED THE SECOND DAY I was in Youngstown. A gaunt, haggard man in his early thirties came to the Saulino house. He too was from Agnone and his name was Luigi Salvatore. He apologized for not having been there the day before to greet me and my *signora,* but he had been too weak and sick. In fact, that was why he was there now.

I noted the feverish glint in his watery gray eyes, the parched yellow skin drawn tight over his sunken cheeks, the unhealthy flush that stained his brow, and I felt pretty certain of his diagnosis.

Luigi went on to explain that he had heard of the great fame of the young *professore,* and he had come to consult me. He had already been treated by a number of local physicians, including, he said, two American doctors (as though that automatically made them superior to our own), one of whom had been a great specialist. Or, at least, Luigi thought he must be great because he had charged him fifteen dollars for an examination, which in 1905 was considered a stupendous fee.

What had been their opinion about his case? I asked. What diagnosis had they made?

On that point, Luigi was vague and confused. But with regard to what they had done for him he was anything but vague or confused. They had done him no good! They had not made him well. If anything, he was much worse now than before he had gone to them. That was why he had come to me. I was his last, best hope. Everybody had said I was a wonderful doctor, a maker of miracles. If I could not cure him, then no one could.

My heart sank. I knew only too well that his case was hopeless. All the doctors in Christendom would never be able to restore Luigi Salvatore to health—or even to keep him alive much longer. If he was ever to be cured, it would need the aid of the only Man of Miracles, whose name—Salvatore—he bore.

Fortunately I would not have to pronounce this dread sentence on him. Although in Italy I was a doctor, in the United States I was still nothing. As yet, mine was merely a "courtesy title." I could call myself "Doctor" Daniele, but until I had been licensed to practice medicine by the State of Ohio, I wasn't legally permitted to treat a sick cat. I explained this to Luigi and told him I was very sorry, that much as I wanted to help him, there was nothing I could do.

I felt guilty. Why, I couldn't understand. I had done nothing wrong; all I was doing was obeying the law. Nevertheless, that look in his eyes made me want to hide. Perhaps in those few days I had been in America I had already become infected with the virus of its damn-the-torpedoes spirit. I don't know. In any case, I knew I couldn't turn him away empty-handed. I had to do *something*—even if it was little more than a mere gesture—to fortify his hope and courage.

I had a pretty good idea what was the matter with Luigi. In fact, I was absolutely sure he was suffering from active and incurable tuberculosis, and that it was in its final stages. But I solemnly listened to his medical history and then proceeded to examine him as best I could with little more in the way of instruments than a stethoscope, thermometer, sphygmomanometer and an eye-ear-nose-throat set. Listening to his lungs and checking his temperature simply confirmed what I already knew.

Naturally I could not treat him or prescribe for him, even had there been some therapy or medicine that might have helped him. There wasn't even any point in referring him to any other physician. He was too far gone for that, or for a sanatorium either. Instead, I gave him a prescription, one that I felt the law would not quarrel with and that, while it might not help his body, might work for the good of his soul. I told him what he needed was "mountain air"—no, not Saranac or Denver; he must have *native* mountain air, the same air he had breathed when he was a child and a young man, the same air that had kept him strong and healthy. He must go back to Italy, to Agnone, to his wife and four *bambini*. At least he would die in peace among his loved ones.

Luigi's eyes glistened with sudden joy. I had given him wonderful advice. He felt better already just thinking about returning home and seeing his wife and children. Yes, his friends had been right. I was a miracle worker. All those other doctors had been fools, or worse. I alone had talked sense and given him sound counsel.

Now I felt more than ever guilty, and ashamed. Native mountain air, indeed! Still, idiotic as it sounded, it might keep alive his dwindling hope and courage long enough for him to return to the bosom of his family and not have to die in loneliness, among strangers.

I saw his bony hand dig into his pants pocket. When he withdrew it a moment later there was something shiny clasped between his fingers. He held it out toward me, his hand trembling. It was a silver dollar.

"No, no, Luigi!" I said. "I cannot take it."

"But, Doctor . . . you have earned it; you have started me back on the road to health."

I shook my head. Again I explained that I was not allowed to practice yet; I would have to go to Cleveland and take an examination, and if I passed it, then——

He pressed the coin on me, insisting that I was entitled to it as my professional fee and that he didn't want to accept charity, even though he couldn't afford to pay me what my skill was worth.

The mere thought of accepting that money—even of touching it—made me feel a little sick. What disturbed me was the thought that if I took his fee, my very first patient in America—indeed, almost my first patient anywhere—would be a man for whom I could do nothing except prescribe "native mountain air" and send back to Italy to perish. I was superstitious enough to believe that under those circumstances that gleaming dollar would be *maledetto,* cursed, and would bring me nothing but bad luck. It was bad enough that my first patient should be someone doomed to die.

But Luigi grew more and more insistent, even a trifle angry, thinking that I was refusing his money because I thought he was a pauper. At first, I didn't know how to wriggle out of it gracefully, without letting him know the real reason for my refusing his money. Then an inspiration flashed into my mind.

"*Vedi, caro Luigi*—look, dear Louis," I said. "You are my very first patient here in America. Among doctors back home it is considered bad luck to take money from your first patient. Now, surely," I went on, giving him a friendly smile and mentally crossing myself for this shining white lie I had just made up, "surely you would not want to be the one to bring me misfortune, would you?"

He shook his head. Of course not. With a little sigh, he put the coin back in his pocket, thanked me and praised me several more times, pumped my hand and departed.

Less than a month later he came back to see me and to say good-by. He was on his way to New York to board a boat for Naples. And not too many months after that, I heard from friends in Agnone that Luigi Salvatore had died, peacefully and contentedly in the arms of his wife, his four *bambini* by his side.

Yet sometimes I wonder about that case. Viewed from a different angle, it might not have been a failure at all. Although I had not cured Luigi's broken body—nothing could have done that at that point—I shall always feel that I succeeded in giving new strength and life to his tired, defeated soul. In the copy of Walt Whitman which my uncle gave me, these lines had been underscored by him:

> *O my brave soul! O farther farther sail!*
> *O daring joy, but safe! are they not all the seas of God?*
> *O farther, farther, farther sail!*

6 : First Office, First Impressions, First Foe

IT WAS ON JULY 3, 1906, that I received my license to practice and hung out my shingle. In the six months between my arrival in Youngstown and my official induction into the army of disease fighters I had carefully scouted the terrain of my future operations. After investigating half a dozen or more possible locations for an office, I rented a suite in a fairly new building on East Federal Street, one of Youngstown's principal thoroughfares. It was situated at the intersection of several important arterial streets that led into highways running to the surrounding suburbs, near-by towns and Cleveland and Pittsburgh, the nearest large cities, both of which were approximately sixty-five miles west and east, respectively, of Youngstown. I was located at a strategic traffic center and would be readily accessible to any and all my patients, even those living at a considerable distance from the central part of town. This, in 1906, was a far more important consideration that it is today; dependent on literal horsepower or primitive automobiles and with poor roads, transportation was a serious problem for any physician.

My choice was a sound one; I did not have to wait long for patients. More fortunate than most young physicians starting practice, within a few months after receiving my license I was already quite well established and was so busy I could hardly spare the time, or energy, to take care of all the new patients who sought my professional services.

From a physician's point of view, Youngstown was an ideal place to practice his art; it was a natural breeding place of disease and accident. The damp, foggy, smoke-infested atmosphere produced a high incidence of tuberculosis, respiratory infections, rheumatism and arthritis, as well as cardiac and circulatory diseases. Crowded, near-slum living conditions contributed to and furthered the spread of all sorts of infectious maladies, sometimes to epidemic proportions. Chicken pox, scarlet fever, diphtheria, measles, whooping cough, grippe and scabies were constant visitors in the homes of the immigrant population. In addition, as a result of the exhausting nature of their labor, there was a rather alarming amount of physical, nervous and mental debilitating disorders. Venereal disease was widespread, and in those days, before the discovery of antibiotics and sulfa, it was a far more serious problem, not alone for the individual but for the community at large, than it is today. And of course, the accident rate was high, because of the dangerous kind of work most of the men were called on to perform.

I knew how to deal with bacteria and viruses. I could handle fractures, lesions and other standard surgical procedures. But when I came up against superstition I was struggling with an elusive, shadowy, yet potent foe. In my case it was somewhat sharper and more intense than with most of my colleagues because my practice, at least during my first years, was almost entirely among people of limited economic means and even more limited education. Until I had established myself in the community, I lacked authority to override the fears and weird notions and old wives' tales of some of my patients. I had to rely on reason, on knowledge, on patient explanation and persuasion, to dispel the fogs and chimeras of ignorance, and they are generally poor weapons in the eternal war on superstition.

Night after night I would come home utterly worn out, tense with worry over some particularly difficult case. I would drag myself home from the office or an outside call at six, seven, eight, ten o'clock, whatever time it would be, and Elvira would always be waiting for me, smiling, gentle, understanding, with never a word of reproach for being late. Dinner would be ready no matter at what hour I arrived, and invariably it would be hot, delicious and well served. How she performed this miracle of timing I never did discover, but perform it she did. And whenever I would be called to see a patient in the dead middle of the night, not only would she not complain at having her own rest disturbed, but when I returned she would be up, waiting to greet me with a cup of hot coffee or chocolate. During all the years of our life together there may have been some occasions when she complained about something, but I cannot remember them. She was the perfect doctor's wife.

At that time another woman came into my life. Her name, as nearly as I can recall it and as accurately as I can spell it, was Skrzynskiewcje, or some similar unpronounceable congestion of consonants. I called her Rose Ess. She was Polish or, rather, of Polish descent, for she was that then rare creature, a second-generation "foreigner" born and reared in Youngstown.

Rose was invaluable. She had a seemingly inexhaustible store of energy, vitality and strength and was keen to extend it on my behalf. Since I was just launching my career and had extremely limited means, I could not afford the large staff that the volume of my practice soon demanded. Rose "tripled in brass," efficiently serving as nurse, secretary and receptionist. She also acted as a sort of combination liaison-intelligence officer, briefing me on many patients, who they were, how much they could afford to pay, what their backgrounds were, what romantic attachments they might have, if any, their personalities, habits, idiosyncrasies, reputations or lack thereof, and any other sundry pertinent information that would be and was enormously helpful to me in treating them. She frequently acted as an ambassador for me, pacifying patients who might have some grievance, calming frightened, nervous ones, laying down the law to stubborn or refractory ones and generally performing the duties of a buffer between my patients and me.

In addition to all of which, however, the greatest service she rendered me was to teach me English. Rose's knowledge of Italian was, at best, meager, little more than a random collection of words and phrases picked up among the Italian residents of Youngstown. She spoke Polish fluently and English that was both correct and American. I, on the other hand, knew no Polish and my English, as I have already demonstrated, was primitive—and that is describing it quite charitably. Elvira and many of my friends questioned my choice of Rose for the job. Their attitude was a "practical" one. Why hire a girl whom I could barely understand and who could barely understand me? Why not hire an Italian who spoke English? That was certainly a logical, reasonable argument. Too much so, as far as I was concerned. Acting on the theory that the best way to learn to swim is to jump into the water, I had decided that the best way to learn English was to be forced to speak it, not occasionally or when I felt like it, but every day and all day long. I had absolutely ruled out hiring anyone who spoke Italian.

Sometimes, as I look back on it, I wonder how I ever did succeed in establishing myself in the United States. The truth of the matter is that I don't think I would have done so without the help of Elvira and Rose. Their patience, encouragement and understanding got me over many a hurdle that would have otherwise thrown me.

Among the practical handicaps that the physician, along with the attorney, must endure is that which very wisely, forbids him to advertise or seek any form of publicity. Here again, so it appeared to me, the American doctor was at a somewhat greater disadvantage than his European colleague, for the European's position and prestige in his community served to spread his renown throughout the area of his practice. In this country the practitioner had to rely on his ability, initiative and personality to stir up "word of mouth" advertising that would bring him new patients. This has always been one of the most ticklish problems in the entire realm of medical ethics. Every physician, being a human being as well as a medical man, has a natural impulse and an economic need for letting the world know that he has a better mousetrap than the fellow down the street. No one can censure him if he tries to make this known discreetly. But the trouble arises when his over-aggressiveness causes him to cross that uncharted boundary that separates legitimate recommendation from advertising.

American advertising was just beginning to stretch its brawny young limbs and industry was discovering how truly sweet are the uses of publicity. The world was witnessing the transformation of John D. Rockefeller, Sr., from a monopolistic monster into an altruistic angel by the magic of that Merlin of the Mimeograph machine, Ivy Lee. It was hardly surprising, therefore, that the immigrant doctor should sometimes be tempted to flirt with this fascinating new medium of self-exploitation.

One afternoon, less than a month after I had opened my office, two young men came to see me. One was enormously tall, straight and skinny, with a gaunt face, hypnotic eyes and an unkempt jungle of black hair. The other was in every respect his diametrical opposite; he was short, squat, almost totally bald and his eyes were little more than two sleepy slits. The big one was named Giovanni Fanfaroni, the small one Tommaso Giordano. They were my first introduction to a type that later came to be known as "racketeer" and of which my compatriots, alas, were to produce far too many specimens.

The tall one, Giovanni, did most of the talking. They had come to see me, he said, because they had heard very good things about me and wanted to help me make money by the bushel.

"That is very kind," I said, noncommittally. "How do you propose to do that?"

"By advertising you," said Giovanni with a bright smile, as if he had suddenly hit upon some great, startling discovery.

I shook my head. Advertising was not permitted members of

my profession, I told him. We were not allowed to publicize ourselves in newspapers, magazines or trade journals.

He merely beamed at me rather patronizingly, and his partner did likewise. Giovanni went on to explain with the air of a patient schoolmaster instructing a backward pupil that what they had in mind was nothing so crude and obvious as that. No; what they proposed was far more clever, far more subtle and effective. Their scheme was *fare una piccola propaganda*—"to make a little propaganda"—in my behalf among our fellow expatriates.

"And how are you going to do that?" I demanded.

"Well, maybe you tell me this," he said, still smirking. "How does any doctor make his business grow fat, eh?"

"By treating his patients properly, so they'll be pleased and recommend him to their friends."

"*Punto!* Precisely!" There was a triumphant gleam in his eyes. "That is how we shall advertise you also."

Now I was mystified. I wanted to know how he intended to accomplish that.

"*Va bene, signor dottore.* We show you."

He buttoned up his coat. He announced that we were now in an imaginary saloon. It was crowded with our fellow countrymen. Among them was Tommaso, leaning against the bar and enjoying a quiet beer by himself. Now Giovanni enters. He spies Tommaso, greets him very noisily, embraces him, slaps him on the back, pumps his hand excitedly and exclaims in utter amazement how surprised he is to see him among the living; he had thought he had died months ago when he was so terribly sick. Now it is Tommaso's turn to speak. He explains, in a loud bellow, that he had indeed been at death's door, but an astounding miracle has taken place and he was snatched from the very threshold. That is Giovanni's cue to demand, "How?"

Before going on to reveal the nature of the miracle, however, Tommaso was to make sure they had attracted the attentive curiosity of everyone within earshot. Then, and only then, he would tell Giovanni about the great healer, the man who could raise

Lazarus from the dead, *il medico magnifico,* that paragon of paragons, Dr. F. Michele Daniele, whose address is such-and-such and whose telephone number so-and-so. Giovanni would thereupon shout lustily that mankind should thank God for giving us such skillful physicians, and he would launch into a rhapsodic panegyric in praise of such noble, unselfish, able, wise, inspired, generous doctors as Dr. F. Michele Daniele.

But suddenly he would check himself and exclaim, "Ah! but you have not told me how much he charged you for this incredible miracle! I'll bet he took your eyes out!" That would then give his associate the opportunity to broadcast how kindly, how charitably, how sympathetically he had been treated by that good, sweet, dear Dr. Daniele, that prince among men, that truly Christian spirit, whose ridiculously modest fee is so much for an office visit and so much for a house visit. Why, it almost made one feel like a beggar or, worse still, like a thief to pay so little for such marvelous care and attention. Tommaso would go on to tell Giovanni how, feeling ashamed at paying such a paltry amount, he had tried to get the doctor to accept *una mancia,* a tip, but had been quietly told this was not necessary; Tommaso had compensated him for his services in truly princely fashion.

At this point in the act, carried away by his grateful emotions, Tommaso would fling a couple of silver "cartwheels" resoundingly on the mahogany and call out, "Drinks for the house! Everybody drink with me to the health of that great friend of mankind, that benefactor of humanity, Dr. F. Michele Daniele!" (In 1905, you could buy a small ocean of beer for two dollars.) Then, after everybody had joined in a ringing toast, *un brindisi,* Giovanni and Tommaso would move on to a saloon in another part of Little Italy and give another performance. For this "propaganda" they asked a ludicrously tiny fee, according to Giovanni. All they wanted was ten dollars a day for the team—plus expenses, of course.

I had to admire the ingenuity of their scheme, for all its rather elephantine obviousness—although actually it was well suited to its proposed audience, on whom subtleties would have been lost.

At the conclusion of the demonstration Giovanni mopped his cadaverous features with an immense red bandanna, gazed at me hopefully, waited to hear me say they were hired. I almost didn't have the heart to tell them I couldn't buy the act; they seemed so eager and so hungry—even Tommaso, for all his plumpness, looked as if he hadn't eaten for days.

I was curious to know more about these would-be missionaries and how they had ever hit upon such a means of earning a livelihood; if earn it they did, and I seriously doubted it. Giovanni, who was still doing all the talking for both, explained that they had come to the United States about a year before in the hopes of practicing their profession with greater profit than back in Italy, but the pickings had been very slim. In fact, they had been practically nonexistent. It did not surprise me to learn that the profession they had practiced at home had been acting. Now, instead of following in the illustrious footsteps of Salvini and Duse, they were reduced to exhibiting their artistry in barrooms and not even getting an opportunity to do that.

I must confess I felt a bit sad about having to refuse their offer. I endeavored to make them see and understand why it was utterly impossible for me, or any other ethical physician, to employ such a device, clever as it was. Besides, almost any doctor who might require that much help to build his practice would certainly not be in a position to pay ten dollars a day plus expenses for their very effective services. And those who could afford it obviously didn't need it. I was indeed sorry to have to give them such a gloomy prognosis, at least insofar as the medical profession was concerned. But it was an extremely ingenious idea. Why didn't they try to sell it to some other field?

They looked extremely discouraged and disappointed. Not only my heart was touched, but my pocketbook as well. I reached into my pocket, took out a dollar and handed it to Giovanni.

Their mournful faces lit up instantly. It was easy to read

the cheerful story that was written on them now. That dollar would provide them with twenty schooners of beer and, what was still more important, twenty free lunches—the better part of an entire week's eating. They departed amid the typically Italian barrage of fervent *grazie*'s and the customary handshaking.

There was a shortage of medical talent at that time in Youngstown, particularly among the Italian-born segment of the population. Before my arrival, the brunt of the burden had been borne by an extremely able, wise, devoted practitioner, Dr. Giuseppe Scarnecchia. He was getting on in years, but even for a man half his age it would have been a crushing task. Ordinarily a doctor will take a rather doubtful view of another's hanging up his shingle in competition. But in this instance, the incumbent was doubly delighted to have me come on the scene—first, because he needed someone to relieve him of some of the load; second, because "Joe" Scarnecchia was that kind of doctor and that kind of man; he didn't have a mean, jealous or selfish bone in his body. Even if there hadn't been enough "business" to go around for everybody, I am sure he would not have resented the appearance of another doctor in Little Italy.

I remember being called one night to examine a nine-year-old girl. She had a rectal temperature of 104.6 degrees; her respiration and pulse were abnormally quickened, and she was in a near-comatose condition. I diagnosed it as acute bronchopneumonia, and I advised that she be sent to the hospital at once.

The child's aunt offered a different diagnosis. According to her, the girl was suffering from something called *sangue gelato al petto,* or congealed blood on the chest. When I told her there was no such disease known to medical science she became purple with rage, accused me of being an "alarmist" and shouted that I was trying to make a big case out of it in order to charge a larger fee. I appealed to the bewildered parents not to listen to her, but she evidently carried so much weight with them that they brushed aside my advice and removed me from the case on the spot. They were also terrified by my wanting to send their daughter to the hospital.

In those days, there was a general fear of all hospitals; among the foreign-born population the very word was enough to produce panic, for it was almost universally believed that once a person went into a hospital he was doomed and would leave it only in a wooden box. This fear was not altogether without foundation. In the first place, hospitals were a good deal more primitive than they are today. The quality of therapeutic and diagnostic technique left much to be desired, as well as the standards of nursing care. Secondly, most of them were pretty grim, forbidding, cheerless places, filled with an atmosphere of pain and suffering and unpleasant smells that called up visions of ghostly operating rooms, hacked-off limbs and blood. But the factor that was most responsible for causing them to be shunned was the very dread and terror with which people regarded them. The more serious the illness, the longer the patient or his family would put off calling the doctor, lest he decide to send the sick person to the hospital. Thus it was a common occurrence for the physician to be called on the case when the patient was *in extremis,* and sending him to the hospital was a last, desperate hope. As a result, the mortality rate in hospitals was abnormally high, because so many people refused to go to them while they still had a fighting chance.

In the case of the little girl with pneumonia, I had no choice but to quit the scene, hoping against hope that Nature and her youthful constitution might overcome the deadly bugs. Medical ethics prevented me from remaining on the case, once I had been summarily dismissed. I did, however, report it to the local health authorities, but before any action could be taken the child was dead. That vindicated my medical judgment, but it didn't make me feel any better about the whole thing. I would have been far happier had she recovered and given her aunt the opportunity to gloat over me, even though it would have surely meant that "congealed blood on the chest" would have thenceforth become permanently fixed in the symptomatology of Dr. Superstition.

Some time after that, I was summoned to treat a very similar case. This time the patient was an eleven-year-old boy named

Riccardo. He was suffering from a severe nephritis. An American physician had preceded me, and he had quite properly ordered the boy sent to a hospital, with precisely the same result as I had had with the little girl. He had been discharged from the case, and Riccardo was given no medical care at all, other than such home remedies as his mother and the neighbor women dreamed up. Finally, as his condition became alarming, they sent for me. I took one look at him and immediately sent for an ambulance. Now the parents made no protest; they knew it was their only hope. But once again it was too late and the superstitious old women and the ignorant womenfolk were able to croak triumphantly that the hospital had claimed another "victim."

That case stands out vividly in my memory. I recall going out into the corridor with his father after Riccardo had died, leaving the mother to weep and moan over the body. The father kept mumbling, *"Non capisco; non capisco—*I don't understand; I don't understand———"

I asked him what it was that he didn't understand, and after some more incoherent muttering, punctuated by sobs and little cries, he told me that he had made a special trip into the woods himself a number of days before to collect various herbs that he brought back home. His wife had brewed them into a kind of tea to which they had added several drops of holy water. This, according to him, had been his grandmother's unfailing remedy for any and all ailments, its formula one of the most guarded family secrets. They had forced it down the boy's throat, and now the father simply could not comprehend why it had failed to work. Never before had it proved ineffective. He was utterly mystified.

Hospitals were not the only thing they were afraid of; many of the most modern medical techniques were looked upon with boundless horror and dread. There was another boy who had been complaining of a "sore throat." It turned out that he had diphtheria. I proceeded to administer the first of a series of antitoxin shots, but the moment I started to sterilize the syringe his mother let out a shriek, sprang to her feet and snatched the glass tube out of my hand.

"No! No! No! You cannot do it!" she cried. "I will never let you do it! Never! Never!"

"But why, *signora?* It is the only thing that can save him."

"Better than that he should die than you should pierce his flesh. It would be a sin!"

Nor could I convince her. I summoned another doctor, who joined his arguments and pleas to mine, but still she would not budge. Under no circumstances would she permit us to give her son the life-saving serum by means of the hypodermic syringe, though she had no objection to our administering it by mouth or by rectum in the form of an enema. This was sheer idiocy, of course. Diphtheria antitoxin cannot be introduced into the body that way, for one thing. And for another, as we tried to make her understand, what difference did it make whether it was by mouth, rectum or through the skin? In each instance it was still an injection. But our words bounced off her like buckshot off a rhinoceros. She only shook her head, kept insisting she would not let anyone puncture her boy's flesh; that was a terrible sin. Why exactly, she never explained, though I suspect it had some association in her simple mind with the Crucifixion.

My colleague and I struggled—not for too long, I'm afraid —to save the boy by some other means. We performed a tracheotomy on him, making an incision into his windpipe so that he could breathe. We racked our brains and medical textbooks to find remedies. But without the antitoxin the child was doomed. Twenty-four hours later he was dead.

Happily, however, all cases involving superstition did not terminate grimly. One of my very first patients was Donna Rachele Lanari, who was a good fiftyish and was built on the generous lines of a wine cask. She complained of tiring quickly and excessive perspiration. I started to go through a routine examination, but she brushed aside my stethoscope. She insisted on being examined by *la macchina,* the machine. When I asked her what kind of machine she had in mind she said the kind that could look inside people. She had seen doctors' ads proclaiming the virtues and supernatural powers of *la macchina,* and her friends had told her about it too.

I patiently explained that, first, only quacks advertised and, second, an X-ray or fluoroscope examination would not be able to reveal why she tired easily and sweat profusely. Nevertheless she demanded *la macchina,* and when I refused to waste her money by sending her to have X-ray pictures taken, Donna Rachele stalked off in a huff and never returned.

Then there was a farmer named Achille suffering from a mild bronchial catarrh for which I prescribed a medicine that cost him only half a dollar. Two days later he was back, complaining that he felt much worse; and when I expressed some slight surprise he said, "How do you expect me to get well on that cheap medicine you gave me?"

I nodded but did not reply, and went over him again. When I had completed the examination I wrote out another prescription for exactly the same medicine, only this time I added something to give it a very unpleasant taste and a different color.

As soon as he left the office I phoned the druggist, told him the situation and asked him to charge my patient two dollars this time. At first he hesitated, said it was an outrageous price, even fifty cents was outrageous, since it didn't cost him more than about eight cents to make. But I insisted that the exorbitant price was an all-important part of my therapy, and he finally consented to soak my farmer.

A couple of days later my patient was back. But this time he was beaming and announced that he had not returned as a patient but as a friend to thank me for having made him well. The new medicine, he said, had done the trick. And he added, "You never get results with cheap things."

Many times during those early years it seemed to me that the least part of my task was healing sick and broken bodies. More often than not I found myself having first to straighten out warped, crooked thinking and to overcome stupid and sometimes deadly notions before I could undertake the treatment of the physical disease itself. It was a discouraging business, having to stand by helplessly and watch people die whom you might have saved. That your own judgment would ultimately be vindicated was the coldest of cold comforts. What joy can you get out of being right, when you have had to watch a child gasping for air as he struggled in the murderous grip of dipththeria or perished from peritonitis because his parents were afraid of hospitals or thought it was a "sin" to pierce the flesh?

There were many moments when, returning wearily in the hushed loneliness of dawn from the bedside of a patient wantonly sacrificed to Dr. Superstition, I was almost on the point of quitting this heartbreaking profession altogether. Why go on? I would ask myself. The ones you make well take their cues for granted and give the credit either to their own "marvelous constitutions" or to their patron saint. The ones you do not make well damn you for an incompetent quack and refuse to pay your fee. Why, then, wear yourself out fighting ignorance and prejudice for the benefit of those who do not appreciate it? Why, then, go on? And in the depths of my despair and fatigue I would not be able to find an answer.

7 : Largo al Dottore

IN MEDICAL SCHOOL we were taught all there was to be known about medicine, and almost nothing about the *practice* of medicine. We studied anatomy, communicable diseases, morphology, surgical technique, psychology, forensic medicine, orthopedics and dozens of other subjects. But we received no instruction in what today would be called human relations and public relations, in how to select an office site, in bookkeeping or in practical ways of building up a practice. Everything was kept on a lofty intellectual plane. Such down-to-earth matters were regarded as beneath the dignity of a university's curriculum. Once in a while, though, one of our professors—generally one who had had some experience in actual practice—might relax and offer us a crumb of useful, everyday wisdom. One such random observation has remained with me for nearly sixty years. I cannot remember anything about the man who made it except that he was professor of gynecology and obstetrics. "To be a good doctor, it is not enough to know medicine," he said. "You must be like Figaro—be able to handle all sorts of odd jobs at a moment's notice."

In half a century of active practice the truth of that statement has been demonstrated to me repeatedly. In my time I have been called upon to act as everything from matchmaker to financial adviser. Of course, this has ever been the traditional role of the general practitioner in a smaller community; and the more he succeeds in winning the confidence, affection and respect of his patients as a man of medicine, the more they will spontaneously turn to him as a man whenever they need advice or help. Frequently, too, pathological and practical problems have a way of overlapping and interlocking, one affecting, controlling or coloring the other. In recent years, this has become known as "psychosomatic medicine" and has even been elevated to the dignity of a separate specialty. But in the old unenlightened days we just accepted it as a matter of course that people's bodies were affected by their minds and vice versa, and gave our patients whatever friendly, practical help we could in our twin capacity of physician and good neighbor.

Nowadays it has become rather fashionable to glorify and extol the humble "hick" G.P. as a shrewd old coot and a successful rule-of-thumb psychiatrist. Forgive me for spitting on the temple floor, but that has always struck me as a lot of pretentious flapdoodle. I think I was a fairly typical "hayseed horse doctor" —perhaps even more so than most American G.P.'s, for being an immigrant myself and practicing among immigrants, I was able to get even closer to my patients than the average small-town doctor. And I suppose over a rather extensive period I did my share of what might be termed cracker-barrel psychologizing, and with a reasonably fair batting average, too. But I never saw any reason on that account for regarding myself as a kind of combination of Dr. Sigmund Freud, King Solomon and Florence Nightingale. Hardly a day passed that we weren't called on to tackle and solve some human problem that had nothing to do with medicine and yet had everything to do with it.

A typical instance—one among hundreds in my own experience—was the case of Tommy Brown. Tommy was a kid of about fourteen. He had been born in Italy but had been brought over here when he was five and, to the naked eye, was a real American boy, without a trace of his Italian origin. His father had become an American citizen and had changed the family name Bruno to its English equivalent Brown. By retaining the

Italian form of his own first name, the result was a rather bizarre combination—Enrico Brown.

I had taken care of the Brown family since I had begun practice and was fairly well acquainted with their general background, history and circumstances. They were by no means wealthy, but Enrico had his own business and was quite prosperous. Nevertheless, young Tommy had an after-school job selling papers so that he could earn some extra money to help pay his way through college.

When I came to look at Tommy I was surprised and puzzled not to find Mrs. Brown waiting to greet me at the door, nor was she hovering at her son's bedside. I made no comment on this extremely unusual situation, however, but asked Rico what seemed to be the trouble with his boy. His description of the symptoms was quite vague—feverishness, aching and general malaise.

I was not able to get much more out of the patient. It was apparent he was suffering considerable pain, but he refused to tell me anything. All he kept saying was that he wanted his mother. When I tried to examine him he pulled away from me and wailed, "Mamma! Where's my mamma? Why isn't she here?"

Between his father, and his elder sister Teresa and myself, I could have forced him to submit to an examination, but I preferred to use gentler methods, if it were at all possible. I took his father aside and asked him where the boy's mother had gone, why she wasn't there with her son.

Rico squirmed and hesitated.

"Out with it!" I snapped. "There's no time to lose. We've got a sick boy on our hands. Where's Rosa?"

Ever since I had got there my suspicions had been growing. Now they were confirmed. Rico's wife had run off with a handsome *mascalzone,* a scoundrel, named Pietro Spinelli, better known around the poolrooms and saloons as Pretty Boy Pete. Rico had no idea where they might have gone. Maybe to Cleveland. Maybe to Pittsbubrgh. Or maybe even to Chicago or New York.

All he knew was that she had disappeared two days before and with her had disappeared every penny he had in the world. They had kept a joint bank account and she had cleaned it out before departing with her lover.

It struck me that Rico was oddly calm and unemotional for one who had just had, as we say, the horns put on him. He was not angry or vindictive. All he wanted was for his wife to come home, and he was ready to understand and to forgive all. But how to persuade her to return? Where was she to be found? He could hire detectives, of course, but that would take time and money, both of which were now in crucially short supply. Or he could notify the police. But that would mean a nasty scandal; thus far Rico had managed to conceal the truth from Tommy and Teresa.

"Rico, we must get her to come back," I said. "I can only do so much for Tommy. Without his mother here I can promise nothing."

"But, Doctor, how can I do it?"

"I have an idea. I'm not sure it'll work——"

"What is it?" His eagerness was pathetic to see, even a trifle embarrassing.

"*Dopo, dopo,*" I said. "Later. For now I want you to tell Tommy his mother is on her way back to him."

He stared at me blankly. "But . . . what if she——"

"Let me worry about that, Rico. You just say to him what I have told you, and say it in a way so he'll believe it. *Capito?*"

"*Capito,*" he said, nodding. "Understood."

We returned to the bedside and his father told his shining white lie, whereupon Tommy, characteristic of his youth, wanted to know *when* his mother was coming home, where she had gone and why she had gone. I confess I felt sorry for Rico as he painfully spun out the web of lies, improvising plausible answers to Tommy's new questions.

I decided I had better step in at this point, before Rico got in too deep. It was obvious that Tommy was satisfied thus far.

"Now that your mamma is coming home," I said to him, "what do you say to letting me look you over and getting you well again for her, eh?"

"*Sì, sì,*" he said.

"Very well. Then we begin by taking your temperature."

"*Sì,*" he said.

Tommy's temperature read 103.9 degrees. His pulse was very rapid, his breathing shallow and his chest sounds anything but encouraging. He complained of headaches and a dull pain at the back of his neck. There had also been some gastric disturbance earlier that day.

I did not like the look of it. The symptoms pointed suspiciously in the direction of polio—or, as it was more generally known at that time, infantile paralysis. It might only be a severe grippe, or influenza, or pneumonia—the onset of all of them is quite similar; that is what made polio such an insidious killer. Nevertheless, I felt it was wiser to be an alarmist and play it safe. I told Rico the boy would have to go to the hospital.

Rico blanched, bit his lip, but did not, as I feared he would, raise any objection. Not so, though, Tommy. He let out a loud howl that he was being tricked; we had promised him his mother would return to him, and now we were shipping him off to the hospital! Rico and I assured him his mamma would come back, and even though he was in the hospital, she would visit him every day, all day long. After some little argument he yielded. Within less than an hour Tommy was sleeping under mild sedation in the quarantine ward, where he would remain until it was possible to rule out the suspected polio—*if* it could be ruled out.

On the way back to my office I asked Rico which newspaper his wife was in the habit of reading. The *Bulletin,* he said.

"*Va bene,*" I said. "Let's go over there."

"But it's closed."

"I know."

"Then why should we go there?"

"*Pazienza! Pazienza!*" I murmured a little wearily, but inwardly rather enjoying the mystification. I could almost feel Rico

itching and twitching with curiosity beside me, but I was determined to keep him in suspense for a few more minutes, knowing
that he would appreciate my plan all the more.

The night city editor (I've forgotten his name) was a friend
of mine. What I wanted him to do was run a small news story
in as prominent a position as possible stating that Tommy Brown,
son of Enrico and Rosa Brown, had been taken to the hospital
with a suspected case of infantile paralysis. Under no circumstances, however, was my name to appear in it. In addition, I
asked him to insert the following personal in the so-called "agony
column" the next day and to continue running it until further
notice:

> ROSA: Hurry home. Your son is dangerously ill. He needs you
> and is calling for you. Bygones are bygones. There is no hatred,
> anger, malice or revenge in my heart. I still love you and always
> shall. If you wish confirmation telephone the doctor. Youngs-
> town 562.

I told my editor friend to send the bill to my office.

Next day the *Bulletin* carried both the personal notice and
the news story, the latter right on the front page and running
in every edition. Rico waited in an agony of suspense and fear
for something to happen, and I suffered along with him. Twenty-
four hours passed without one word from Rosa. The personal
appeared for the second day. Rico and I still hoped, but it was
beginning to be against hope. If she saw the notice, then surely
she must have seen the news story on the previous day, and if
she refused to respond to that—well, then it really was hopeless.
Perhaps Rico was better off without her. Perhaps God in His
infinite wisdom had chosen this painful means of freeing Rico
from a heartless woman, a mother without love and without pity.

It was edging toward dusk. I had just completed my daily
office hours. The last patient had departed, a sixty-seven-year-old
man with an incongruous case of measles. Tired, beaten down,
discouraged, I sat by my desk brooding, pondering the perfidy
of mankind, but more especially its feminine component, and

struggling to find some way to explain to Tommy why his father and I had failed to make good on our collective promise to deliver his mother. I was awakened from my dismal reverie by the jangling of the phone. With a weary sigh I reached toward it, expecting to be summoned to yet another bellyache or sore throat that would brook no delay. The voice at the other end of the wire was a woman's and unfamiliar. *"Pronto,"* I muttered into the mouthpiece. "Dr. Daniele speaking."

"Doctor, this is Rosa Brown." She explained that she had not seen the paper until rather late the night before; that was why I hadn't heard from her sooner. She had been traveling ever since. Yes, she was back in Youngstown. She was calling from the station; she wanted to make sure it was true, what had been printed in the paper. She was afraid it might be a trap. With all the sincerity, eloquence and power at my command I assured her it was true, that she need have no fears. Rico was a fine man, loyal, loving, utterly devoted to her and her children. He was incapable of holding a grudge or seeking vengeance, richly as he might deserve it.

I could hear her sobbing. *"Sì . . . sì . . .* I know. He deserves someone better than me. I am not good for him——"

"He loves you and needs you," I told her. "That's all that matters—and the fact that your boy needs you even more right now."

"Tommy!" she cried. "Tommy!"

I told her to hang up and wait right there for me, that I would rush over to the station and pick her up and take her straight to the hospital. She asked me to let Rico know, but I said that could wait till she had seen Tommy. He was my first and immediate concern, and having her back would be the finest medicine I could give him.

Later that night, over a bottle of the best *Asti spumante* in Youngstown, Rosa tearfully recited her story. I hadn't wanted to hear it; after all, it was none of my business; my sole interest in the matter was getting her back so that my patient would have a better chance to get well. But Rico and Rosa both insisted I remain and listen. Hadn't I played a part in it myself, and a very important part too? So I stayed and heard her tale, which was not a pretty one, though quite human.

She and her lover had gone to Cleveland, intending to stay there a few days and decide where to go next. But the train had barely left the station when she felt a wave of fear, of doubt, of guilt and panic, surge up within her. For suddenly, altogether inexplicably, although the man she loved to distraction, who loved her so, was seated right by her side, suddenly she experienced a terrifying sense of aloneness. This feeling of loneliness, rather than diminishing as Youngstown and the past faded further and further into the smoky haze, increased, grew more intense and more oppressive, and with it came a piercing nostalgia. It puzzled her; it bewildered her; it filled her with dread and misgiving. Her lover first sought to cheer her by telling her tasteless jokes and making love to her, but she was too perturbed to respond, besides being rather shocked and disgusted by what she instinctively felt was bad taste. After a while he became annoyed with her "coldness" and accused her of being a "bum sport," turning his attention to studying the racing tip sheets he always carried in his pocket. The rest of the romantic abduction was accomplished in peevish silence till they reached the outskirts of Cleveland.

The tension eased somewhat after they had checked into their hotel and settled in their room. But Rosa found it difficult to show the same spontaneous enthusiasm and affection she had shown previously; she tried hard to pretend it, but such things not even the most skillful actress can conceal for long. Pietro soon sensed there was something definitely lacking. (It has always struck me as curious that women, for whom love is a vital part of their existence, are rarely successful in dissembling a love they do not feel; whereas men, to whom it is more of an incidental embellishment, are generally far better deceivers.) During a grindingly long evening divided between a dull dinner and an even duller show, the lovers sulked in their tents, and Pietro came out of his only long enough to blow up at her because she had bought a Youngstown paper at the hotel newsstand. Why couldn't she forget about that dump? he wanted to know. If she really loved him, she would put her old life behind her forever.

Till that point Pietro had been paying for everything himself, and quite handsomely too. Now, as soon as they were in their room again, he demanded money from her; he didn't even ask to borrow it, Rosa said; he just said, "Gimme," and started to grab her purse. But she was too quick for him, snatching it out of his grasp and handing him ten dollars. That made him furious, and a bitter, snarling quarrel followed which ended by her giving him twenty-five dollars; that left him still furious but twenty-five dollars richer.

Besides disgusting and depressing her, this sordid argument completed the process of disillusionment and reawakening that had begun the moment she boarded the train in Youngstown earlier that day. Now, for the first time, she clearly realized that her great romantic passion had not died; it had never really existed at all. What she had thought was love had been, on her part, mere infatuation and, on his, a cold, calculated scheme to get his hands on the money she had told him she had in the joint bank account. And if she might still have had any lingering doubts as to the true nature of his feelings, he dispelled them then and there. After abusing her in the vilest gutter language for being miserly, cold, selfish, stupid and dull, he clapped his hat on his head and stormed out of the hotel.

Alone, yet strangely less lonely than when she had been with Pietro, Rosa picked up her newspaper and began to read it.

"It was like God was talking to me Himself," Rosa told us. "There, in that dark hour, cut off from everybody who loved me, deserted, disillusioned, I looked at the paper and suddenly a name shot out at me, and then all I knew was that my Tommy was sick and that I must go back, if it was true. Yes, it was God that made me buy that paper, that made me fight with Pietro. That was how He opened my eyes to the truth."

She could not bear the thought of spending another moment

in that room or even in the hotel. She had dressed and gone to the terminal. But there were no more trains to Youngstown until the late morning. She spent the remainder of the night sitting in the waiting room, dozing fitfully on a bench.

When daylight came, however, she began to have some second thoughts about returning. Would Rico really forgive her? Or was he saying it in the newspaper ad just to get her back? And what about the children? Did they know about her? She could not bear the thought of facing them if they did. Then it occurred to her that the whole thing might be a clever trap, so that Rico could then obtain a divorce from her or maybe even have her arrested.

But the thought of her child lying sick in a hospital, perhaps dying at that very moment—that was more than she could bear. The personal notice might be only bait to tempt her into the snare; but her instinct told her the newspaper story was true. She believed it; she had to; she couldn't afford not to believe it. She decided to return and phone the doctor and find out if Tommy really was sick.

That was her story. An old, threadbare one, a staple of pulp magazines and trashy, sentimental novels of that era, as it was later to become a staple of movies, radio, soap operas and television tear-jerkers. It did, however, possess one novel, refreshing twist—especially "refreshing" to Rico—in that Rosa not only returned herself but so did most of Rico's hard-earned money, save for the twenty-five dollars Pietro had managed to get.

In this case, life proved kinder and gentler than fiction, which requires that every sinner be chastised and made to pay for his sin. To be sure, Rosa must have paid for hers a thousand times over in the form of bitter self-reproach. But happily Rico did not bear any grudge or seek to revenge himself in any way. Rosa's momentary blunder did not do any lasting injury to their marriage; if it had any effect at all, it seemed to strengthen the ties between them.

As for Tommy, my patient, who was the one I was chiefly concerned with, he had been his own best physician and had prescribed wisely and well for himself; for his mother's return proved to be miraculously effective medicine. I kept him under observation for a few more days, until we could positively rule out polio and decide that it was intestinal flu.

This was only one among literally hundreds of extracurricular odd jobs I have been called on to perform in the course of trying to make people well. A worried patient is always a difficult patient. It has seemed to me that once you accept that fact, you are then obligated to use every legitimate means in your power to locate and wipe out the cause of that worry. Not all of my colleagues agreed with me.

To that end, therefore, I set out to develop machinery that would make it easier to accomplish these purposes, just as I had bought instruments and office equipment when I began to practice. I became one of the most active "joiners" in Youngstown. Before I was through, I was a member of all sorts of Italo-American societies, fraternal groups, social clubs, civic-betterment associations, patriotic organizations, masonic societies and lodges. I collected "contacts" as other men collect stamps, books or pictures. Not only did I never miss a chance to do a favor; I eagerly sought out opportunities to do them. My politician friends called this "fence-building" and "fence-mending," and it has always struck me as a very apt metaphor. I soon got to be quite expert at it.

Once I pulled one of my more prosperous patients, a contractor named Franco di Meo, through an extremely serious siege of illness. To celebrate his recovery he gave an enormous dinner for his seemingly limitless army of relatives together with a sizable task force of friends, business associates, public officials and even total strangers who had apparently wandered in off the street. As the one who had been chiefly responsible for making this *festa* possible (with an assist, of course, from Nature and the good Lord), I found myself seated with Elvira on the flag-draped, flower-bedecked dais.

Italian banquets are never considered complete unless they are finished off with a generous helping of bicarbonate and oratory, both achieving exactly the same result. Having had some little experience of them, I should have known that after we had stuffed our bellies with heavy, indigestible food, our heads would be stuffed with heavy, indigestible speeches. Moreover, I should have also known that inevitably I would be called on to render unto di Meo those things that were di Meo's. But being modest and innocent, or just plain stupid, that horrible thought never entered my mind. It therefore came as quite a shock to hear, through a smoky, drowsing haze of afterdinner stupor, the toastmaster pronounce my name in a loud, ringing voice and to hear it followed by a burst of applause with which were mingled a few feeble *Viva*'s. For a second or two I just continued to sit, beaming foolishly at the crowd, nodding my head. Then I felt Elvira's elbow digging into my ribs and heard her whisper, "Get up, *stupido,* and make a speech!"

Speech-making is like betting on horses: it becomes an incurable disease if you succeed the first time. Once I found that I could get an audience to sit still and listen to me, I was doomed. And as I did with everything else, I applied myself to public speaking in grim earnest, studying voice production and projection, improving my enunciation and enlarging my vocabulary. My speech-making was not exactly a waste of time, as it gave me renewed confidence and an added sense of power and authority; and this I found useful. It aided me in my constant battle with superstition. Now when some fool wanted to fight deadly germs with a string of garlic, or refused to go to the hospital, or insisted upon my consulting with a witch doctor, some wrinkled old *strega,* I had little difficulty getting my opinion listened to and obeyed.

Then, too, from a purely material standpoint, it served as a form of discreet advertising beyond the pale of possible criticism by members of my profession, eagerly watching for the slightest infraction of "medical ethics." To be sure, there was plenty of grousing and grumbling in private about "this fellow, Dr. Daniele," who was trying to "grab all the business in town." For the most part, these complaints came from the non-Italian practition-

ers, though I learned that one or two of the newer, younger
Italian doctors joined in the discordant chorus. There was some
vague talk about denouncing me to the County Medical Association, but nothing ever came of that, since there were no conceivable grounds on which to base a charge against me.

But I was ambitious—and I was young. I hadn't yet crossed
the thirty-year mark. In a few, short years I had succeeded in
establishing myself in a foreign land. I had built a practice that,
while not a rich one, still provided me with a more than adequate
income and caused me to be envied by a great many of my colleagues. I had won a position of respect and some prestige in the
community. Best of all, I could look back on what I had achieved
with the deep satisfaction that comes from knowing you have
created something entirely by yourself, by your own hard work,
by your own skill, determination and dedication to your task.

Yet such is the perversity of human nature that I was not
happy. Having conquered my tiny world, I yearned for new triumphs. I sought new fields to cultivate and master—not necessarily greener fields, but new ones, more difficult and challeng-
ing ones. Everything I had thus far achieved now seemed insig-
nificant and easy. The time had come, I felt, for me to prove
myself to myself. I must win success upon a strange, unfamiliar
battlefield where I would be fighting alone, unaided, unknown.

8 : A Fallen Woman Helps Me Rise

IT HAS BECOME a commonplace of every success story, whether real or fictional, for the hero to "owe everything" to the pure love of some pure woman. Mine is not exactly a success story; say, rather, it is just another human story. Surely I can say that while I don't owe *everything* to Elvira, I do owe her a great deal. Not so much because she contributed to my success, but because she contributed mightily—to my deep, inward happiness. For my peace of mind, the flowering of my spirit, I shall always be in debt to her.

I fixed for myself in rendering this account of my life an Honesty Is the Best Policy program. Now I confess that I was helped over the next big hurdle in my career not by the "love of a pure woman" but by the frendship, respect and admiration of what used to be known as "a fallen woman"—to be exact, the madam of one of the best sporting houses in Youngstown. It happened this way. . . .

Early one summer's evening I received a phone call at home right after dinner. It was a lovely, moon-drenched night and Elvira and I had planned to take a spin in the merry Oldsmobile, which I had bought only a few months before to replace my horse and buggy. The call was from a Mrs. C. Aubrey, who wanted me to come right over to see her. No, this wasn't Mrs. Aubrey speaking, the voice said; it was the maid. When I asked what was ailing her mistress she said it wasn't Mrs. Aubrey who needed me but one of the girls, and Mrs. Aubrey would tell me herself what was the matter when I got there. She gave me the address—in the best residential section of Youngstown—and asked me how soon I could come. I told her in about half an hour. She asked me to make it sooner, if possible. I promised to hurry.

I guess I have always been a simple-minded innocent. Although I had been a resident of Youngstown for a number of years and thought I knew pretty much everything that was going on, it never dawned on me that Mrs. C. Aubrey was also the notorious Madam Caroline and that the elegant address I had been given happened to be that of her popular establishment. Even had I been much less naïve, I don't think I would have realized it, because, quite frankly, I was too excited at the prospect of treating my first non-Italian patient. Put it down as snobbery, if you like; but like every other foreign-born practitioner in town, I had for long been casting a covetous eye on the non-immigrant portion of the population. It wasn't entirely for social reasons, however; what was of far more important consequence was the economic angle. Moreover, breaking through the wall that separated the native Americans from the immigrants meant that a physician's professional abilities were given tacit recognition and approval not only by the wealthiest but by the most influential and worthwhile members of the community. It meant that he had crossed over to the Right Side of the Tracks, that he was "made" and his future assured. It is the way of the world, and those of us who would remain in it, working and living in it fruitfully, must accept its ways.

I grabbed my bag, bustled into my linen duster, cap and goggles, without which no sane person would have thought of riding in the Merry Oldsmobile of the time. I struggled for nearly five minutes cranking my monster, clambered aboard and took off, quite literally, in a cloud of dust. That night I hung up a record for the course, covering the few blocks from my house to Mrs. Aubrey's in precisely seventeen minutes flat!

The house was a spacious, handsome one for that period, an excellent specimen of Benjamin Harrison baroque, overrun with curlicues, scrollwork, garish stained glass and meaningless minarets erupting at odd intervals from its shingled roof. It stood in a rather large plot of ground and well away from all its neighbors, as if it had been quarantined—as, in a way, it was. The deep, broad lawn in front was littered with a small herd of iron deer, and the house itself was partly concealed from the street by several enormous old trees that now cast it into deep shadow. The wide porch, running the full length of the front and around two sides, was curtained by cascades of lilac and wisteria that seemed like ghostly white veils in the moonlight. The house was completely dark save for a pale yellow radiance streaming from the opened front door. Somehow, I couldn't help shuddering as I gazed at it. It looked like a house of death. What would I find within it?

Mrs. Aubrey's maid was waiting for me at the door. She was a pretty Negro girl with soft skin the color of coffee taffy and sparkling eyes and a gentle, friendly smile. She wore a neat black dress short enough to show a pair of slender ankles, and over it she had on a frilly white maid's apron, and a white cap to match perched pertly on her head. She greeted me politely yet cordially and ushered me into a large, richly furnished sitting room. Its walls were covered with dark-green damask on which hung a number of huge paintings, each one illuminated by its own electric light. The furniture was upholstered either in silk brocade or in tapestry. A thick Persian rug covered almost the whole floor. The entire room breathed wealth, position, power. It filled me with a deep sense of contentment.

In the far corner sat an elderly, distinguished-looking man in an expensively tailored business suit. He had white hair parted down the middle and a white mustache elegantly trimmed and waxed. He was reading a newspaper, and as I entered the room he gave me a quick, uninterested glance and went back to his paper.

The maid waved me to a gilt armchair and said, "Won't you

sit down, Doctor? Madam won't be long. She'll see you right after she sees this gentleman here." She smiled again and disappeared into the dark, silent depths of that enormous mansion.

Who was this other man? And what was he doing there? And why should I have to wait until he had finished talking to Mrs. Aubrey—if that was who he was going to talk to? I had been asked, virtually ordered, to rush there as fast as I could. Whatever the nature of the mysterious malady might be, it had been impressed on me that it was urgent. And now that I had arrived, instead of being hurried up to the sickroom, I was pushed into a chair and told to wait my turn. One might have thought that *I* was the patient sitting in the doctor's waiting room.

Five, ten, perhaps fifteen minutes passed in this fashion. A deathly stillness filled the entire house, broken only by my companion's wheezy adenoidal breathing and the occasional crackle of his paper as he turned a page. I looked around the room to see if I could find some reading matter, but without success. I tried to kill the time by studying the pictures, most of which belonged to what has been aptly termed the Cow-in-the-Field School. They were completely uninspired and uninteresting daubs that had, I was sure, cost a great deal of money.

Suddenly, without a sound, the maid reappeared; she didn't walk into the room—at least, so it seemed to me; she just materialized out of nowhere. I didn't even realize she was in the room until I saw her glide past me and go toward the man in the corner. She bent down and whispered something in his ear. He lowered his paper and I heard him mutter, "High time . . . high time . . ." Then he got up, carefully folded the paper and followed the maid out of the room. I never saw him again.

Now I was alone. I had exhausted whatever little interest those insipid paintings had to offer, and that left me with nothing to do but sit and think and wait. For what, I had no idea. Nor why. The old fellow had gone off with the newspaper; I had eyed it suggestively as he was folding it and walking out of the room, but he had ignored my mute appeal or else had not noticed it at all.

More time passed. In reality, it probably wasn't much more than ten minutes, but it felt like an hour. I kept looking at my watch, growing more and more impatient and angry. Several times I considered walking out—indeed, was almost on the point of doing so. But there were a number of reasons why I didn't. It meant too much to me to break into the charmed circle of Youngstown's best people to throw away an opportunity like this, for one. Then, too, my curiosity was aroused. What was the meaning of all this huggermugger? Why had I been told to hurry over as fast as I could, then made to cool my heels? And there was still another reason: I had no idea where the maid had put my cap, duster and goggles, and without them I could hardly have driven home.

Presently I heard footsteps and then muffled voices somewhere in the distance behind me. It was a man and a woman. I couldn't make out what they were saying, but one of the voices sounded vaguely like the elderly gentleman's. Then, quite clearly, I heard the woman say, "Oh, thank you, sir!" And she laughed. I didn't hear the man laugh, though. Just an indistinct growling kind of rumble. Then footsteps again and the sound of a door closing. And again silence.

Now, more than ever, I was puzzled and intrigued by all the mysterious mumbo jumbo. Why had the elderly gentleman—if it was he—sneaked out of the house, apparently by a secret exit? Or was it just the back door? Even so, why hadn't he departed by the front door, as he had probably entered? And what had he come for? I wondered what sort of important business he might have had with Mrs. Aubrey that took precedence over a doctor who had been sent for so urgently.

My somewhat bewildered reflections were interrupted by the return of the maid, who again suddenly materialized out of thin air. She was, as usual, smiling. In a confidential whisper she said, "Madam'll see you now, sir." I got up, and I must have looked as irritated as I felt, for she added apologetically, "I'm sorry you had to wait so long, Doctor. But the other gentleman was here ahead of you." I was about to ask her why she had insisted on my hurrying, but I decided there was no point wasting more time.

She led me down a dimly lit hallway and stopped in front of a door that had a small gilt metal crown on it. She tapped on it discreetly and a clear, silvery soprano called out from inside, "Come in! Come in!" The maid opened the door for me and I caught the smothering scent of sandalwood.

The only way I can describe the room is to say that it reminded me of fluffy pink whipped cream. It was furnished as a boudoir—all frills and lace and soft satin—and yet there was something incongruously businesslike about it. This was caused by a massive roll-top mahogany desk in one corner of the chamber on which was a litter of papers, account books and similar stuff.

A few feet in front of the desk, placed as though to highlight the startling contrast still more, stood an oversized chaise longue—the largest, in fact, I have ever seen anywhere. Its frame was made of elaborately carved wood painted a creamy ivory color, and it was covered in *couleur de rose* watered silk which, in turn, was covered by the equally oversized body of a woman, swathed in a filmy negligee of some kind of deep crimson stuff and trimmed with ostrich feathers of the same shade. Although she was of behemoth proportions—she must have been well over six feet tall and weighed close to three hundred pounds—yet there was an astonishing feminine charm, softness and grace about her, even a certain incredible daintiness, as though some insane potter had deliberately fashioned a mammoth Dresden doll. As is the case with so many stout people, especially women, she had features which, while not beautiful, were quite pretty; about the only word I could employ to characterize them is to say they were "cute." It was the face of a little girl—sweet and stupid, yet with a hard, cold shrewdness concealed beneath the lovely surface. Her complexion was on the florid side, though it was a little difficult to tell how much was complexion and how much was makeup. Her rather disproportionately small head was covered by a mass of thick, soft yellow-gold hair, which she wore carefully curled. Her best feature was her eyes. They were startlingly dark, and had rather the effect of giving the lie to the childish innocence of the rest of her face. They were lustrously beautiful, also piercing and crafty. Her figure, for all its immensity, was paradoxically voluptuous and shapely.

I approached her couch, feeling as if I were floating, rather than walking, as I trod the thick, soft rug.

"Mrs. Aubrey?" I said. "I'm Dr. Daniele."

She smiled softly and held out a surprisingly small, delicate hand and said, "Yes, I am Mrs. Aubrey—though most folks in Youngstown know me better as Madame Caroline."

. I guess I must have gulped, for her smile became a chuckle and she added, quite pleasantly, "I hope, Doctor, I haven't shocked you——"

"Why . . . no, no, you haven't," I stammered, a bit confused.

"Now, don't tell me you didn't know who Mrs. Aubrey was or what kind of a place you were coming to, Doctor!"

I felt silly and embarrassed having to admit I hadn't had any idea. That produced a hearty, good-natured laugh this time; but there was absolutely no trace of mockery or scorn in it.

"Well, Doctor. I certainly got to hand it to you," she said. "I don't know what kind of a medicine man you are, but I do know you ain't no four-flusher. Most jokers would sooner be caught playing with themselves than admit to being so innocent."

I shrugged. "I've found the truth pays in the long run, even though sometimes it hurts, Mrs. Aubrey."

"That's the way I figure it too. By the way, d'you mind not calling me Mrs. Aubrey? Oh, that's my name, all right. But it sounds so kind of—well, formal. Most everybody calls me Carrie or Madam Caroline, if they want to be real elegant. Sometimes they call me other things, too," she added with a big friendly grin. "But we'd better not go into that, Doctor. I don't want to shock you again."

I laughed. "I think I'll manage to get over it, Mrs.——I mean, Madam Caroline."

"I'm sure you will. Now, I suppose you're wondering why I sent for you, eh?"

"I've been wondering ever since I got here over half an hour ago."

"Oh, yes! I must apologize for keeping you waiting so long. But you know," she said, a twinkle in her dark eyes, "business before pleasure. Though this is business, too, I suppose. I just don't believe in keeping customers waiting."

"It's a sound policy in any business, or . . . profession," I said. "And now, supposing you tell me what seems to be troubling you?"

"Oh, no, Doctor! You've got the wrong end of the stick. There's nothing troubling me—leastwise, nothing that *you* could fix. It's one of my girls needs looking after." I coughed nervously and she went on quickly. "Of course I understand this ain't exactly your line of goods. But my regular man went out of town or got drunk, and I thought somebody had better have a look at Millie——"

"How did you happen to pick me?"

"Why, I just called a friend of mine down at City Hall— maybe we'd better not mention no names—and he said for me to get you; they don't come no better—that is, provided I could get you to take the case, he said."

"That explains the Mrs. Aubrey business," I said.

She grinned again. "Guess it does, Doctor. But it ain't too late to back out, if you want to."

I agreed to handle the case, but I wanted it clearly understood that I wasn't signing on as house physician. Madam Caroline nodded briskly. She rang for the maid and told her to take me upstairs. She was to bring me back after I had examined the girl.

What I had seen of the lower portion of the house was luxurious, rich and comfortable, albeit of doubtful taste. The upper regions were bare, ugly, cramped and severely utilitarian. They looked exactly like what they were: a sex factory. The maid led me down a long, faintly lit corridor lined on each side with wooden doors. All of them were closed, but from behind them came a variety of weird sounds testifying to the fact that Youngstown's knighthood was in full flower.

We stopped at a door halfway down the corridor. The maid knocked on it and opened it without waiting for an answer. The room was precisely what it appeared—a crib. It was not more than a few feet wide and two yards deep. Its faded wallpaper was innocent of any adornments, and its only furniture a narrow, rusty iron bed, a small table and a chair, both of which were painted a dirty gray. The only illumination came from a single gas jet turned so low that I could barely make out anything in the room.

There was a girl lying on the bed. The beautiful young prostitute with a heart of gold has become a stock figure of fiction, drama and cinema. Reality is, of course, quite another thing. Even when a girl enters the ancient profession with beauty and youth, within a few years she becomes not old but merely ageless and her appearance utterly nondescript. It is almost always impossible to tell whether a seasoned practitioner is young or old, attractive or ugly. There is something about their trade that seems to have the psychological effect of reducing them to a sort of nonentity. In time all of them become featureless, colorless, impersonal machines almost totally devoid of any but the most superficial human emotions, incapable of responding to anything other than mere physical, animal sensations. As for their having "hearts of gold," though I could scarcely qualify as an expert, I am strongly inclined not simply to doubt it but positively to disbelieve it. From the little I know of them—still being as honest as I can be, and speaking only from my observation and experience with them as a physician—I should say that professional sex purveyors, male as well as female, are in business for whatever the traffic will bear and not for love or sweet charity. If they ever did happen to have a "heart of gold," it was long ago left in the hockshop.

I am unable to say whether the girl I examined was old, young, middle-aged, pretty or ordinary. As far as I could see she was nothing more than a female human being with no distinctive features of any kind—except that she was sick and suffering greatly. A cursory examination was sufficient to tell me she had a severe gonorrheal infection, a far more serious matter in a woman than a man, particularly in that anti-antibiotic era. It was well advanced, and I felt that the best place for Millie was a hospital, where she could receive the frequent irrigations and other treatments accorded in those days.

I returned to the boudoir-office and made my report. I was prepared to encounter the customary resistance to sending the girl to the hospital, especially since it meant losing one of her workers. But Madam Caroline surprised me; not only did she not object, but she volunteered to foot all the bills and told me to get Millie a private room, twenty-four-hour nurse attendance, and everything I thought she needed in order to get well. "Get her the best room in the house, Doc," she said. "I don't give a damn how much it costs!" I assured her I would be personally responsible for Millie's care, that I would look after her as if she were my own daughter. Madam Caroline snorted scornfully. "I'd rather you looked after her like she was your sweetie. Some of the pappas I've known——"

Then she asked me how much she owed me for the visit and I said two dollars, my regular fee at that time for a house call. She gave me a long, hard look. I thought she was going to complain that it was too steep. I was about to explain that that was my standard charge and, besides, I had spent a great deal of time just waiting around. She reached over to a box on a table alongside the chaise longue, took out a cigarette and lit it, exhaling a long, slow funnel of blue-gray smoke. Then she said, "Doc, you're an awful big chump."

"Why?" I asked, genuinely puzzled.

"A visit like this is worth a five, at least. And most medicine men would soak a cathouse madam ten because they know there ain't a damned thing we can do about it except pay. You're just too honest for your own good. Do you mind handing me that wallet over on the desk?" I brought it to her; it was a man's wallet, made of the finest leather and fat with greenbacks. She took out a five-dollar bill and gave it to me. I started to give her the change, but she waved the money away and said, "Around here, Doc, I'm the one who sets the prices on everything."

"My fee for a house visit——"

"I don't give a good goddamn *what* your fees are. If I thought you was asking too much, I'd chop it down, and if I think you ain't asking enough, I'll pay you what I figure it's worth." I started to protest, but she rolled on relentlessly. "Save your breath, Doc. Nobody ever won an argument from a madam in her own house, and you ain't going to win one now. Your price for this visit is five bucks. And let me warn you about another thing." She pointed at me with her cigarette. "Don't send me no piker bill for taking care of Millie in the hospital. Understand? She ain't no charity patient and I ain't looking for no bargains. Not when it comes to doctors and hospitals."

I promised her I'd be very careful not to be gentle in my charges. And the curious part of it was, I think, that I worried more about that bill than any other I ever submitted. I doubled all my normal fees, then added 10 per cent to "grow on" and held my breath, afraid that this time she would let out a howl because I had "soaked" her. But the very day that she received it her maid appeared in my office and handed me a thick envelope. Inside it, on perfumed pink letter paper, was a note on which was scrawled: "Dear Doc, 'Tain't enough. You're still a chump." Accompanying the note was a wad of crisp new currency amounting to exactly one-third more than the total of my bill.

Out of this incident grew a strange friendship. That first visit convinced her, as I later learned, that if I was nothing else, at least I was an "honest quack" and not a "bloodsucker." Then, when I had finally got Millie well again after very nearly losing her, she was convinced that I knew how to "fix the plumbing" as well as be honest. From then on Madam Caroline was my most devoted admirer and most ardent booster. I never treated her or any of the members of her female academy again; as a matter of fact, I never saw her again, but every so often I would get a friendly note from her, wishing me well, sending an anonymous contribution to one of the charitable organizations I was interested in, inviting me to drop in and "have one on the house" or conveying Christmas or birthday greetings—the last invariably accompanied by some rich, handsome gift.

But what was of considerably more importance and value to me was the good, strong push she gave me into the heart of Youngstown's Chosen People. I didn't know it at the time—it wasn't until long afterward that I learned about it—but it was largely as a result of her adroit and subtle propaganda in my behalf, and her, shall we say, immoral support that my professional fortunes were advanced.

Madam Caroline's establishment was the top-drawer institution of its kind in town and as such attracted a definitely superior clientele. Her patrons included important city officials, judges, bankers, executives and other similar worthies who were invariably referred to in the press as "leaders of the community." Many of them had a high opinion of her, respecting and admiring her for her honesty, forthrightness and good sense. It was by no means an uncommon thing for a man to drop in to her place just for a visit, a quiet drink and some intelligent talk, and nothing more. Many a notable had been known to go to her with some particularly thorny problem and seek her advice, for she possessed that all-too-rare ability of seeing things clear and seeing them whole, in addition to being in a position to give disinterested, objective counsel.

Madam Caroline sang my praises to one and all, painting in the most glowing colors my honesty, my integrity and my skill. (I must confess that when I heard about it I blushed and wanted to hide because of my embarrassment.) To all who would listen —and even to some who wouldn't—she recommended my services, but gave what was undoubtedly the most remarkable warning in the entire history of medicine: be very careful, she told them, not to let me *under*-charge them.

Within a few months I found my services in constantly greater demand. I felt I was at last coming in sight of the goal I had set for myself, and a feeling of smug self-satisfaction and even pride began to flood my soul. I had finally "arrived"—or so I believed. But perhaps there was one point about which I was in error: perhaps I was mistaken about prostitutes not having "hearts of gold."

9 : I Examine Myself

DURING MY STUDENT DAYS I had frequently witnessed the death of patients in the hospital. They invariably moved me deeply and aroused my pity, as a human being. As a physician, or an embryonic one, however, they never touched me in the slightest. The responsibility or the guilt, if there were any, belonged to someone else, to the eminent *professori* who had treated these cases. At first I was startled and baffled by their seeming indifference to these tragedies; then as time passed, I recognized that this was the proper way for doctors to behave and maintain a "professional" attitude. Patients were not to be regarded as people but merely as "cases," what seemed cold, inhuman detachment was actually scientific objectivity. What I failed to perceive or sense, of course, was that my professors *had* to remain impersonal and impassive, or risk hamstringing themselves. But it was to take many years before I was to find that out for myself.

Late one night about eight months after my only visit to Madam Caroline's bagnio, I was awakened by a long-distance call from Ellwood City, a small town about twenty-five miles across the Pennsylvania line. It was from a Dr. Mumford, a G.P. whom I had met on one or two occasions, mostly at meetings of the Mahoning County Medical Association. He told me he had a serious case of serofibrinous pleurisy and would like me to come out and have a look at his patient, an Italian woman named Franzetti.

The request rather surprised me. I was not a specialist in chest diseases, or any other specialty. Why should he wish to consult with me rather than with a chest man, of whom there were plenty at the time in Cleveland and in Pittsburgh, which were no further from Ellwood City than Youngstown? I suggested this to him and even mentioned the names of a couple of excellent men, but he explained it was not so much a matter of consultation—he felt quite certain of his diagnosis—as it was of simply having another doctor on the case, particularly an Italian, to sort of back him up and give him moral support. This I could readily understand and sympathize with; it was very much as if I were treating an American patient and wanted an American doctor's help.

But when I arrived on the scene I found that was not quite the picture. Dr. Mumford didn't propose that I should assist him in the case; what he wanted to do was to turn it over to me completely; he would withdraw from it and I would take over. This surprised me, and the hollow reasons he advanced for this unusual step were anything but convincing. It required no occult insight to discern what lay behind it: he was afraid Mrs. Franzetti might die, and he was trying to shift the responsibility off his own shoulders onto mine.

I told him he had nothing to fear; the woman's husband and family were decent, sensible people and would not hold him to blame if anything happened. But it was no use. He seemed to have some strange fear of Italians, regarding them as savages who might turn on him and tear him to pieces, maybe even devour him like cannibals. I know this sounds rather silly, but it was quite true. He was actually in mortal terror of what might happen to him if his patient did not pull through. After I had talked to him a few minutes and realized the state of his nerves, I saw that his usefulness on this case was at an end; indeed, I felt he would be more a hindrance than a help. Reluctantly I agreed to take his place.

Serofibrinous pleurisy is a disease characterized by a bacterial infection, as a rule, of the pleura, the membranous tissue that envelopes and protects the lungs. Inflammation results and the pleural cavity, the space between the inner wall of the covering sheath and the lung proper, becomes injected with blood and, in some cases, pus. Sometimes the amount of fluid that accumulates can become so great that it compresses the lung, driving the air out of it, and expands the lung sac so much that it brings dangerous pressure on the heart. When that occurs it is necessary to remove the fluid surgically by tapping the lungs and draining off the liquid, an operation known as thoracentesis. This is a painful procedure, since it cannot be performed under a general anesthetic, only under a local. In Mrs. Franzetti's case it became twice necessary for her to submit to it, and she did so bravely and uncomplainingly.

She was not too old a woman in spite of the fact that she had six *bambini*. I doubt that she was much over thirty-five. Under normal conditions, she might have been considered a young, strong, healthy woman. But like so many Italian women, excessive and needless child-bearing had weakened her constitution and made it all the harder for her to battle the disease. For two weeks I struggled by her side, aiding her in her courageous fight. At least once each day I drove to Ellwood City to see her—and a thirty-five-mile trip in those days was nothing to be taken lightly. On several occasions I kept vigil over her throughout an entire night. By the eleventh day her condition began to appear hopeful. Her husband, a shoemaker by trade, started to rejoice and to broadcast glowing reports about *il dottorissimo,* the miracle-working medicine man who had snatched his wife out of the very claws of the dark angel. I did my best to discourage his over-eager optimism, pointing out that his Stella was far, far from being out of danger and that it is always a risky business to tempt fate in that fashion. But as she continued to show steady, though slow, slight improvement each day he kept up his hosannas.

During the next four days her recovery went on, and I was even starting to feel glad I had let Dr. Mumford persuade me into taking over. My reputation would climb even higher, if I succeeded in bringing Mrs. Franzetti back to health.

On the morning of the sixteenth day I got a phone call from Alfredo Franzetti. His voice was shrill, trembling, near-hysterical. I could barely make out his frenzied south Italian dialect. Only two words could I actually understand—*Presto!* and Stella. But they were enough to tell me that what I had dreaded from the very beginning was now happening.

By the time I had raced out to Ellwood, Stella Franzetti was beyond my help or that of any other mortal. She was still alive, but her breathing was harsh and rasping, her eyes glassy. Within five minutes after I arrived by her bedside she expired with a soul-piercing, heartbreaking groan. It almost seemed as if she had clung to the last shred of her existence until I got there so that I could see for myself how a patient dies, so that I could experience the agony and anguish of witnessing with my own eyes what it really means to lose a "case."

Her husband collapsed, and it was some time before I was able to restore him to consciousness. Meantime, the children clustered around their mother's body, crying out to her, the younger ones begging her to "wake up," the older ones kissing her lifeless hands and sobbing. The womenfolk of the neighborhood, discovering the tragedy by some sort of telephathic agency, flocked into the death chamber, adding their wailing and keening to the hysterical symphony.

Now suddenly the realization came to me of what those doctors back in medical school must have suffered inwardly when their patients failed to reach the finish line. Grim questions tormented my brain. What had I done wrong? What had I not done that I should have done? Had my diagnosis been correct? Had I been right in accepting Dr. Mumford's diagnosis in the first place? But I had tapped her lungs twice and each time drained off an enormous amount of pus-filled, bloody liquid. That certainly bore out the pleurisy diagnosis. Still, there might have been other complications. Had I taken every possible precaution to guard against them? And had I employed the proper therapy? Had I explored every conceivable avenue?

These questions, plus a score of others just as torturing, whirled through my mind during the rest of that damnable day and all of that sleepless night. For hours I lay in bed beside Elvira, twisting and turning, struggling with sleep that would not come, trying to banish thought and memory—in vain, in vain. Elvira, that sweet angel of understanding, lay sleepless next to me, knowing, sensing, what I was suffering, eager to help me, to comfort me, to dispel my guilty self-reproaches, yet realizing that she was powerless to aid me, that this was one battle I must fight out by myself. Throughout that endless night she never asked me a single question or uttered a single word, waiting there in the dark for me to turn to her and speak to her, to seek her advice and opinion. Yet I was helpless to utter a word, to give her the smallest sign that would invite her into my heavy-laden heart.

Finally I could stand it no longer. I slipped out of bed and went down to the library. For perhaps the fourth or fifth time that day I reread everything in my medical treatises dealing with pleurisy, trying to find some clue, even the faintest hint, as to what I might have done wrong or had omitted to do. I almost wished I might discover *something* that would give me tangible cause for accusing myself, no matter how damning it might be; at least it would put an end to this flickering uncertainty and fear. A real enemy I could combat; but against shadows I was impotent, unarmed.

For hours I remained there, in the shrouded gloom of the library, pondering what had happened. The irony, the tragic, melancholy irony of the situation, filled me with bitter laughter. The recollection drifted back into my mind of all those many times in the past when I had prepared myself for just such an event. Every doctor does so; he must. Though he may be the greatest physician since Aesculapius and a miraculous healer second only to Jesus, still he must face the fact that he, as all other mortals, is subject to that inexorable law of averages and that, soon or late, through no fault, no shortcoming or neglect on his part, he must go through the agonizing ordeal of "losing a case." How many times I had told myself I would some day have to pass through that fire! And how many more times I had told myself that when that moment came I would accept it with philosophic calm, with detachment, with what I called "perspective."

Certainly, at this juncture the last thing I was able to do was to regard the first death among my patients with cold scientific detachment. All my long years of careful preparation, my careful cultivation of the philosophic temper, had vanished in that instant when I heard Stella Franzetti utter that last, terrible moan.

Later that day the undertaker brought me the death certificate to be signed. My hand was shaking as I filled it in and scrawled my name across the bottom of the document. Although I had been in active practice for a number of years this was a new and anything but pleasant experience. I was therefore rather startled when the undertaker suggested that I attend the funeral. Somehow that struck me as if the hangman were to pay a condolence call on the family of the condemned man. But the undertaker insisted it would be a great act of Christian kindness and one that would be deeply appreciated by the dead woman's husband, children and family.

My first impulse, of course, was flatly to refuse. The thought of having to kneel beside the open casket and pray, to gaze upon the face of the patient whom my small store of skill and science had failed to save—this was an ordeal I felt I could not bear. But the undertaker insisted it was my duty whether I could bear it or not.

On the morning of the funeral I drove to the Franzetti home. The parlor was filled with mourners. In the center of the room stood the unadorned black wood coffin, a tall lighted candle at each corner. Its top was open. Stella Franzetti lay within, her pale hands clasping an ivory crucifix, her thin features serene. I knelt beside the bier, crossed myself, muttered a prayer, then rose and forced myself to look at her.

A sudden hush fell upon the room. I could not help wondering how many of the mourners were silently accusing me of her death. It seemed as if every eye had been turned on me. I shuddered. I slowly walked over to where Alfredo and his children were sitting. In a low voice I offered my condolences, and he nodded vacantly and motioned to me to sit down beside him. Instantly the tension that I had sensed in that airless chamber seemed to vanish.

I made an attempt, a rather feeble one, I fear, to talk to the widower. We exchanged one or two polite, empty words, but I found it almost impossible to think. The overpowering sickly stench of those masses of flowers and the oppressive, seemingly deliberate atmosphere of crushing grief and gloom paralyzed my brain. I just sat there in a kind of stupor, gazing out into the shadowy room, waiting for the procession to start for the church where the funeral Mass would be said.

Suddenly the sillness was broken by a piercing scream. Everyone turned to face the one responsible for this harrowing outburst, a fat, gross woman of about fifty who rushed to the casket, dropped to her knees like a poleaxed cow and began wailing and weeping, all the while pounding her breast, pulling at her greasy gray hair and calling on the Holy Virgin and all the saints to witness her sorrow. Then she leaped to her feet, bent over the coffin and planted a loud, slobbering kiss on the lips of the corpse.

For the first time Alfredo Franzetti appeared to come alive. *"Bugiarda!* Liar!" he snarled under his breath. Then he whispered to me that the woman was Stella's cousin, that she had always hated her, and his wife had never had any use for her or trusted her. She had never done a kind, decent thing in her entire life, but always at funerals she carried on this way.

Now the amateur Duse began to sway and shake. I was about to get up and go to her aid, but Franzetti pulled me back into my chair, whispered, *"Piano! Piano! Piano, caro dottore!* Take it easy! Take it easy, dear doctor!"

She heaved a rib-cracking groan and collapsed in a neat heap.

Not a person stirred to assist her. No one actually laughed; no one even so much as snickered or smiled; yet I could sense a collective inward guffaw explode in the silence of that house of mourning. After observing this performance for a moment, everyone turned his attention to other things, and the prima donna, realizing she had lost her audience, climbed back on her feet with another mighty groan—this one for herself and quite sincere—and disappeared into the kitchen, where those of a somewhat less funereal bent were bravely trying to "keep up their spirits" with generous applications of food, *vino, grappa* and brandy and were enjoying considerable success in this effort.

We had barely finished with this solo performance when a little old man appeared. He was hardly more than five feet tall, and an enormous bushy gray mustache bulged from the middle of his shriveled face. He was half bent over, and it seemed as if the weight of that massive foxbrush was pulling him down. In his arms he clutched a huge newspaper-wrapped bundle.

I naturally wondered who he might be. More particularly, I wondered why he should be hauling a large package to a funeral and what might be inside it that was important enough to warrant bringing it with him. He approached the bier slowly, solemnly—I might even say it was stately—and then did not drop but, rather, drifted to his ancient, rheumatic knees, lowered his head until it nearly touched his clasped hands and prayed in a barely audible whisper for perhaps five minutes or longer.

A deep, almost reverential hush had fallen upon the whole room as the old fellow paid his final devotions to the departed and prayed for the eternal peace of her soul. The first somewhat comic impression he had created gave way to one of sympathy and respect as he walked toward the casket and knelt beside it in worship. But now, as if deliberately desiring to dispel this mood of reverence and pity, he started to unwrap his package, his quivering, arthritic old fingers fumbling with the string, the paper rattling and crackling and exploding in that deathly stillness with all the nerve-jangling violence of a machine-gun fusillade. At last, after what seemed a whole hour, he succeeded in getting the parcel opened. Like so many rabbits hypnotized by a snake's eye, we watched him, holding our breath, waiting to see what would come out of that bundle.

With trembling hands he held out a pair of scarlet bedroom slippers and a brand-new royal-blue man's shirt toward the coffin.

"Per favore, Stella cara," he said in a low, husky voice, gently, almost tenderly depositing the slippers and shirt in the casket. "I beg of you, Stella dear, take these with you to that blessed place to which you are going. There you will find my poor, poor son, Antonio. Last night he came to me—in a dream—in a strange, black dream—and he was as when he came into the world, all naked and ashamed. He begged me for something to hide his shame before all those angels and holy saints up there." He paused—the effect, I was sure, was not calculated, but it was none the less dramatic and electrifying—and I almost expected to hear Stella answering him. "Please, Stella—please give him these for me."

He broke off abruptly. For a moment he stood there, gazing pleadingly at the dead woman as if he were waiting for her to say whether she would or would not deliver his gift for him.

Two women went up to the old man, gently took him by the arm and led him into the next room. He made no protest and no attempt to resist. He just gave Stella a final farewell look and whispered, *"Addio . . . addio . . ."*

Presently the undertaker appeared with his professional pallbearers. The casket was closed and carried to the horse-drawn hearse. On foot, as is the custom in Italy, all of us followed it to the church and, when the Mass was over, to the cemetery and back.

At the graveside watching Alfredo and his little ones bid good-by to their loved one was one of the most pitiful scenes I had ever witnessed. It was not that they cried, or carried on, or actually did or said anything. That was just it. Their total lack of outward emotion made the parting all the more poignant. They simply stood there by the head of the open grave, a small group clustered together, alone, apart from the rest of the sobbing, sniffling mob of family and friends, staring down into that ultimate pit, motionless, silent, dry-eyed, their dead-white faces expressionless and numb and yet in some curious, indescribable fashion eloquent with pain and loneliness and eternal heartache. Then suddenly, the smallest of the six orphans waved her tiny white hand in farewell and a sliver of a smile flitted across her lips. I turned my eyes away and blindly rushed out of the cemetery.

All the way back to town I brooded over poor Stella and her untimely end. As I drove back to Youngstown by myself I brooded still more, again asking myself if maybe I had not made a terrible mistake. Was I really meant to be a doctor? Perhaps I had been deceiving myself during all these years. Perhaps I had just been lucky so far in not having had any other patients die. Perhaps I had instinctively let Nature play physician to most of my cases, and had taken and received credit for at least half the "cures" she had actually effected. For, as most honest practitioners will admit, most patients will get well by themselves if left alone, and about all the doctor can do is to make them feel more comfortable and sometimes speed their recovery.

Had I really any gift as a healer? Had I any real "call"? That day I wondered . . . wondered and doubted.

10 : A Crusade Is Joined

TROUBLES ARE LIKE WOLVES: they travel in packs. When Stella Franzetti died I braced myself for the new blows that I knew were sure to come. I was not mistaken.

A few months before that unhappy incident one of the most joyous events in my entire life took place—our first child was born. What can I, or anyone else, possibly say to describe the thrill, the deep sense of fulfillment, the kind of drunken rapture that seizes a man at such a moment? I imagine that a poet or a painter or a composer experiences the identical emotion when he completes a work. With this, he tells himself, he has cheated oblivion and guaranteed his immortality—though I must admit I cannot honestly say that that was how I felt at the very instant that I learned a son had been born to me. I was too much excited, far too much relieved and overjoyed, to know exactly how I felt or what I thought. Those rather toplofty ideals about immortality, oblivion and creative fulfillment came later—a good deal later, I'm afraid.

Most people have the notion that doctors take such things in stride and are much less affected by them than laymen are. Nothing could be less true. If anything, I think we become more upset and nervous than others, for a number of good reasons. In the first place, doctors generally avoid treating members of their own family, since it is almost impossible to maintain an objective attitude toward the patient and keep clear of emotional involvements that can distort one's normal professional judgment. Thus the physician finds himself thrust into an ironic and frustrating position: although he may possess all the knowledge and skill in the world, combined with the utmost love and devotion, yet he must stand by helplessly and watch, and hope, and pray, just as if he were the most ignorant clod on earth.

Then, too, his medical training and experience serves only to intensify, not to lessen, his own anguish. He knows, he feels, he anticipates, every pain and ache and symptom the patient is suffering, and he suffers right along with her. Whereas the uninformed layman can only imagine and guess the agonies endured by his loved one, the doctor knows them intimately. Thus his torment is double: first, as a husband, father, brother or son; second, as one familiar with every step in the development of the disease.

Elvira's confinement was mercifully easy and she gave birth to a fine, healthy boy whom we named, among other things, Joseph. Elvira wanted to use the Italian form of the name, Giuseppe, but I insisted that since we were in America and were going to remain here, our son should have an American name, not an Italian one.

Toward the end of June, 1907, Joseph got sick. He ran a low-grade fever and appeared to be suffering from a mild respiratory infection. I gave Elvira some medicine to give to him and he began to improve. I was particularly busy at that time, going through one of those cycles that doctors go through when it seems as if everybody had decided to get sick at the same moment. I was working literally night and day, barely getting a chance to take my shoes off when I would be summoned to another patient. So, true to the ancient adage about the shoemaker's children, little Joseph did not get all the medical attention he should have.

Early one morning as I dragged myself into the house from a call, Elvira was up waiting for me. This was rather surprising, for she had long ago accustomed herself to sleeping while I was out working. The expression on her face immediately warned me there was trouble. Joseph was much worse.

I rushed to the nursery. His temperature had shot up danger-
ously. It was 104.4 degrees; pulse and respiration were very
rapid and his breathing shallow. Stethoscopic examination of his
lungs revealed the presence of *rales*—a kind of rattling sound—
at the apex of the lungs and in the bronchi—the forked branches
of the windpipe going down into the lungs. All the symptoms
pointed to pneumonia. Without further delay I called one of
my colleagues, who hurried over, made a quick examination of
the infant and confirmed my tentative diagnosis.

I wanted to take Joseph to the hospital, but Dr. Houser shook
his head. The child was much too sick to be moved. He advised
getting day and night nurses instead. Elvira protested; if her
baby needed nursing, then she was the one to do it. Houser and
I explained that this was something special, that Joseph's condition was so grave that it required the utmost professional skill,
and that furthermore the strain on her would be too great. She
insisted she could do it and begged us not to call nurses; there
were tears in her eyes as she pleaded with me. It broke my
heart to do it, but I had to place my duty as a doctor above my
feelings as a husband and ride roughshod over her wishes.

Nowadays, even with the potent aid of antibiotics, sulfas and
modern therapeutic methods, pneumonia is still a serious disease.
But half a century ago it was a deadly one, and all those concerned with combatting it had just cause for fear and anxiety.
Elvira and I now climbed our Calvary together as we waited
tensely, helplessly, afraid for the illness to reach and pass its
crisis. Her agony was made even greater and sharper because she
was forced to stand by and watch while strangers fought for the
life of her precious *bambino*. Mine was increased because I could
not desert my responsibility to my own patients and had to go
on holding my regular office hours and making my rounds just
as if I had no private cares of my own.

Then Joseph's condition worsened and Dr. Houser said he
would like to call in a specialist for consultation. Of course I
instantly agreed. He summoned a chest man from Cleveland—
his name escapes me now—who concurred in both the diagnosis

and the treatment completely. There was nothing left for us to do but put our trust in Nature, God and our small store of skill, and wait . . . wait . . . and wait some more.

The crisis came on the third day and our waiting came to a swift, sudden end. Joseph took a sharp turn for the worse. Soon after midnight, during the early hours of July 6, he closed his tiny brown eyes for the last time.

In quiet moments most of us ponder how we would meet various unusual and crucial situations, were they ever to arise in our own lives. I imagine they would try to acquit themselves with dignity, courage and honor, and no doubt they are sincere—or at least as objective as anyone can be about himself.

Now I found myself face to face with the greatest, sternest, most forbidding situation I had thus far encountered in my twenty-eight years of existence. All my resolution to be calm and courageous melted away like butter on a hot stove. I wasn't merely crushed; I was ground down into dust, all my fine, shining defenses decimated. I stopped living, merely going through the motions of my daily routine as though sleepwalking or in a post-hypnotic trance. To this day, I have no recollection of what happened during the months following our loss. I suppose nothing untoward occurred, else I would have found out about it. My instincts and nerves, guided by years of conditioning, must have taken over the management of my thought centers, reflexes and impulses.

This was, of course, Nature's way of providing my tired mind and bruised spirit an opportunity to rest and recuperate. Sometimes this kind of "sealing off" process takes more violent forms in some persons, especially when the emotional shock is sharper, more intense. More disturbed personalities will suffer severe nervous breakdowns, and when there is an organic brain defect Nature mercifully removes the broken mind from all contact with the excruciating realities of life. I was more fortunate. I was permitted to continue to perform all the normal, outward functions of life while my convalescent mind remained in a state of suspended animation.

Nature, I suppose, is the supreme hypnotist, just as she is the supreme physician and surgeon. It was exactly as if I had been placed in a deep trance immediately after Joseph's death and, while I was in it, was ordered to carry out certain specified actions after I would waken from the profound slumber and was seemingly conscious, although still under the hypnotist's suggestive influence in what is termed the post-hypnotic trance. Presumably, I might have gone on in that state indefinitely, but Nature, skillful mesmerist that she is, knew when it was time for me to return to the world of reality and provided a signal to rouse me from my healing sleep.

How many patients I may have treated during that misty-memoried period I never knew. Fifty, sixty, a hundred, maybe more—I cannot say; I don't know. By great good luck I had no mishaps, apparently, since I did not find myself on the receiving end of any malpractice suits. Then one day I got an urgent emergency call to look after a woman down in the worst slum section of town. It was a man who phoned me, her husband, I gathered for he kept shouting frantically, *"La mia moglie muore!* My wife's dying!"* I tried to find out what her symptoms might be, but he was so excited that all I could make out was a shrill jumble of words, some in Italian, some in Sicilian dialect, some in a bastard mixture of English-Italian. I felt fortunate that I was able to find out where I was supposed to go.

Any doctor who has had a fair amount of experience in general practice soon learns what might be called the three cardinal principles of sound G.P.: one, never take too seriously the home-made diagnoses volunteered by the patient or by his relatives or friends; two, do not get alarmed unduly when you are told it is a "matter of life or death"—there are people to whom the smallest twinge of bellyache or a bad cough spells death; third, keep your shirt on at all times. It will therefore be understood why I did not get quite as wrought up as my patient's husband, though I certainly did not dawdle getting to her bedside.

But a strange thing happened to me as I drove over there that sunny afternoon. I was rolling along at about twenty miles an hour (a pretty fair clip for those days) down the main street of Youngstown. It was rather crowded and I was watching the traffic carefully. Then it happened. It was as though a veil had been lifted from my eyes—no, it wasn't even as substantial as a veil; it was more like a film. In reality, it was nothing visible. Rather, it was more a matter of everything taking on a new clarity and sharpness. Not alone as far as my sense of sight was concerned. My hearing also had become keener. In an instant all the street noises had got not so much louder or clearer, but intenser, more vibrant and alive. They seemed to have gained an added dimension, a depth and substance they had not had a second before. I think perhaps the best way to describe what I mean is to say that everything I saw, and heard, and touched, and smelled, had an impact that had been lacking ever since the day my son had passed away. I had an awareness I had not had for months.

When I arrived at my destination five minutes later (the entire episode took place in a matter of seconds) I found that my patient's husband had not exaggerated one bit. If he had been inaccurate at all, it was in the direction of understatement. The sight that greeted me as I stepped into that dark, foul-smelling, filthy hovel shocked and repelled me, for all my years of experience in operating theaters, dissecting rooms and surgical wards.

The woman I had been summoned to see was another of those ageless Italian women who might have been thirty or seventy and who was completely worn out from excessive child-bearing. Her face was haggard and drawn, the skin a chalky, dead white, her eyes staring glassily at the ceiling. She was in coma.

But the thing that startled me was not the woman. It was the bed. The rumpled, ragged sheets were dyed a dark, purplish red. For a second I thought that was their actual color. Then it flashed into my brain that they had been dyed, all right—by the woman's blood. She had suffered massive hemorrhaging, and a quick examination revealed the cause. I tried to halt the flow of blood there, but it was quite impossible. I summoned an ambulance, had her rushed to the hospital and up to an operating table. I tried to locate the ruptured blood vessel in her uterus and tie it off to stop the bleeding. But it was too late. The terrible, criminal damage had already been done. The woman died on the table.

Afterward I questioned her husband. I wanted to know who had been responsible for this piece of butchery. Who was the doctor—if such an assassin could be given that honorable title—that performed the abortion? He stammered that it was no doctor. His wife had done it to herself.

I didn't believe him and told him so, but he insisted it was true, swearing it by half a dozen saints, and I knew it was useless to try to learn the identity of the murderer from him. For some incredible reason, known only to him, he was determined to protect the so-called doctor who had killed his wife. For all I knew, maybe he wanted her done away with, though he sobbed and wept.

But I was equally determined to discover the doctor's identity, if I could, and I attempted to get it out of him indirectly. If she had aborted herself, I asked him, why had she done it?

"*Per carità, signor dottore!* For heaven's sake, Doctor!" he exclaimed tearfully, pressing the fingers of both hands into a tight pyramid and shaking them back and forth pleadingly. "Can you not understand why she did it? Why she *must* do it? Eight *bambini* we got now. Three is dead before we go from Italy— and is too much, too much! One dollar a day I get when I work; only I do not work all the time; sometimes I do not work two, three, five weeks maybe. Two of my *bambini* work—one boy he is thirteen, the other he is eleven—between them they bring home three, four dollars a week. Even so, I cannot put food in all those hungry little mouths. Sometimes some of them must go hungry with me. How, then, am I to feed yet another? *Per l'amor di Dio*—for God's sake—tell me how I could have done it! It's easy for the priest to tell us, 'Go make *bambini,* lots and lots of *bambini!*' It's easy if you only have to put words in their mouths! But he does not have to put food in their mouths! No! That he leaves to me. That is not his worry. He is concerned only with our souls, not our bodies. But the Christ on the Cross to whom he prays, *He* was concerned with the bodies also. Did He not give His disciples bread and fish and wine?"

He paused, eyeing me fiercely, apparently expecting me to take issue with him. When I remained silent, he went on in a loud, belligerent tone that was almost a shout. "I tell you, Doctor, I am happy in a way my Anna is dead. Now she can be at peace, at rest. Now she cannot bring more *bambini* into this world to go hungry and naked, to be miserable, to die even before they have lived—and make the priests happy. No! No! It is much better so! Much better! I am content, very content, *molto, molto contento!*" He drew in his breath sharply. He glared at me as if I were dressed in priestly black. Then he snarled, *"Abbasso i bambini! Abbasso i preti!* Down with babies! Down with priests!"

It was hopeless to try to get the doctor's name out of him; that much was plain. And since I didn't want to get involved in an argument with him—though actually there was little cause for argument so far as I was concerned—I walked away.

As if to underline the significance of this incident, in case I was so stupid and dull-witted as to miss it, two days later I was summoned to see another patient who provided a dramatic contrast to this victim of the tragic misconception of conception. Thanks to my slightly shopworn angel, Madam Caroline, the Evans family, the wealthiest in Youngstown, had been referred to me as patients. In addition to being extremely rich, they were also one of the oldest families in town and the acknowledged leaders of society. I was called to look after their only son, an eight-year-old lad named Bobby.

As befitted their means and station, they lived in a huge mansion filled with rare antique furniture, old masters, rich oriental rugs and precious *objets d'art.* In the sickroom I found two nurses, Bobby's governess and both his parents, the nurses professionally cool, the others fluttering about like nervous hens.

There was nothing seriously wrong with the boy. He was running a not-too-elevated temperature and there was some congestion in the lungs, though nothing to become alarmed about. I prescribed some medication and told them I would stop by next day to have another look at him. By then he was greatly improved and I discontinued my visits. His parents were a trifle concerned about this, thinking that I wasn't giving Bobby as much attention as his illness and their wealth warranted. But I never believed in making unnecessary calls merely for the morale value they might have on a patient's family. This may or may not have been bad "business," particularly when dealing with the rich, who frequently judge a professional man's abilities by the *amount* of service he furnishes rather than its quality and results. I had to live with myself, however, and I had to abide by my principles, no matter what it might cost me in terms of worldly success and material gain.

These two calls, one hard on the heels of the other, made a profound impression on me. It was not the appalling economic contrast between the Evanses and that poor Italian woman murdered by an abortionist, nor between their magnificent mansion and the wretched hovel inhabited by the immigrant family. That was the obvious but rather superficial contrast. What struck me far more forcibly and far more deeply was the vast difference between them simply as people, as human beings, as two families.

On the one hand were the Evanses, richly blessed with the world's goods, secure, influential, leaders in the community to which, over the span of several generations, they had made many important, constructive contributions. The Evans progeny consisted of three children—Bobby and his two older sisters—enough to constitute a well-balanced family, carry on the line and provide companionship for each other, yet not so many that any of them should suffer from neglect, want, lack of care or affection and, yes, spiritual hunger.

On the other side of the picture were the dead Italian woman and her husband, whose total yearly income probably never came to more than $150, if that much. They were unable to feed or clothe themselves adequately, and the only shelter they could manage was a dark, stinking hole that a typhus-loaded rat would have scorned. Yet in a matter of some ten years, they had spawned twelve—no, I cannot call them children—twelve organisms, eight of which had somehow, through some whimsical quirk of Nature, managed to survive, though how many would ever reach maturity was problematical. If they followed the pattern of most such families, five of them would be very lucky to live to celebrate their twenty-fifth birthdays.

Why? I asked myself. Why must this be so? The Evanses, who could easily afford to have ten children, had three, but those three would be given every means and opportunity to develop as individuals and to make a maximum contribution to society. The Italian immigrants, who could hardly afford one child, had produced a brood of two-legged creatures, not one of whom had been furnished with even the barest, flimsiest weapons with which to fight the grim battle of life. What the cause of this insane paradox was I knew, alas, only too well; but what the reason for its existence might be—that was something I could not comprehend, would never be able to comprehend if I lived to be as old as Noah.

Of course, I knew my Italians were Catholics, and devout ones—at least, I felt sure *la signora* must have been. And I knew the Evanses were members of some Protestant communion. I was—and still am—Catholic too. Maybe not the most faithful one in the world, but at least I know and believe in and have always tried to practice the basic tenets of my religion.

I knew also the Church's position with regard to the question of birth control. For years, like so many of my Catholic colleagues, I had comfortably and conveniently glossed over it. Even while I was still in Italy I had begun to have my doubts and misgivings about this cardinal principle of the Catholic faith. To be sure I knew that it did not specifically advocate or encourage the leporine proliferation of children. Its official position was that it did not oppose "natural" birth control; by this it meant that if a husband and wife did not desire a large family, they were perfectly free not to have one by practicing continence —that is, by avoiding sexual intercourse except at such times when they actually wanted to increase their family. But they were forbidden to interfere by any artificial means either before, during or after the sexual contact with the process of conception and fertilization that might result therefrom. Such interference was branded a "sin against nature" and viewed in the same light as various so-called "abnormal" sexual acts, homosexuality or any other deviation from what Church and State have decreed to be the norm.

In theory, this may be convincing and logical. But as with so many, if not most, theories, it is divorced from reality and fails to reckon with what has facetiously come to be known as "the facts of life." Even in the years before I came to the United States I started to become aware of the great, dangerous gap that yawned between the neat ecclesiastical theory and the hard, unyielding actualities of human existence. It was all well and good for the priest, who had felt a "call" and had married Christ, to preach continence and self-discipline. He had his compensations, some of them spiritual and noble, some of them not. But for the strong, healthy, young man and woman, vibrant with life, overflowing with love and devotion, throbbing with passion, this was a cold, barren, frustrating doctrine, a doctrine that was utterly impossible of fulfillment because it was contrary to every law of their nature. To tell human beings that these desires, these instincts and drives, are put there solely for the purpose of mating, of producing offspring, and for no other purpose but that— this, so it seemed to me, is to make a carnal mockery of one of the most ennobling and beautiful experiences that man can possess. To forbid a husband and wife the joys of intercourse except to breed, reduced human beings to the level of beasts who copulated only when the female is in heat and the male's sperm can fertilize her ova. Such an attitude was, I felt, gross and ugly; it robbed human love of all its poetry, its beauty, its tenderness and spirituality, of all its human qualities.

It struck me that the Church viewed the economic and sociological implications and effects of its doctrine with a lack of realism, honesty and ordinary good sense. Because only a microscopic minority were capable of practicing the self-denying continence it preached and because the incontinent multitudes were too terrified by the threat of excommunication and eternal damnation, Italy was being drowned in a sea of *bambini*. Whereas other countries were producing coal, steel, wheat, gold, textiles, chemicals, munitions, she was pouring forth a never ending, constantly swelling stream of human beings. This was her principal industry and her chief commodity for export; unfortunately, however, it did not serve to tip the balance of trade in her favor.

The priests, who were not faced with the problem of feeding hungry bellies and clothing tiny naked bodies, took a comfortable, cheerful view of the increasingly critical question of overpopulation. After all, even granting that many women gave birth to more children than could possibly be supported, only a percentage of them, and a rather small percentage, at that, managed to survive. Actually, so ran the argument, the overproduction was more apparent than real, for not more than 50 or 60 per cent, at most, of the total crop remained. Thus, if birth control were to be permitted, the result would be drastic *under*-production and Italy would soon find herself faced by a steadily shrinking population, as France was. But this neat logic overlooked one salient fact: the Italians are a vigorous, prolific people, and for every child who died before reaching the age of twenty-one, two or perhaps three were born in its place.

To anyone with eyes in his head and feelings in his heart, the pitiful and destructive evidences of unrestricted intercourse were clearly in front of him wherever he went. There was not a city, not a town, that did not have its foul, filthy slums crawling with dirty, half-starved, ragged children, all of whom looked years older than they were. And the mothers of those youngsters! Prematurely aged, worn out, exhausted, physically and spiritually bankrupt from years of serving as baby factories.

Much as I wished to follow my Church's teachings in this as in all other things, the solemn oath I had taken to serve Hippocrates and Apollo compelled me, finally, to study and evaluate this problem by the clear light of science and knowledge instead of by the hazy, mystic glow of priestly dogma and faith. These ideas, as I have indicated, germinated for years before coming to flower. In fact, it really wasn't until the day that I went to see Bobby Evans that they crystallized and I was able to say: "I am in favor of birth control and I am opposed to indiscriminate, promiscuous breeding."

Today such a decision could be easily implemented. In 1907, however, it was a far more difficult proposition. The birth-control movement was still unorganized in the United States and Great Britain; indeed, at that time it was rather more like a secret, underground terrorist conspiracy—particularly in the eyes of its enemies—than a philosophy and a way of life. In 1877, Annie Besant and Charles Bradlaugh had been prosecuted in England for selling a pamphlet, *The Fruits of Philosophy,* by Dr. Charles Knowlton, which advocated and described various birth-control methods. Out of this grew the Malthusian League for the purpose of furthering the spread of information about birth control, contraceptive techniques and the ever-increasing peril of excess population. In 1881, the League was established in Holland and later in Germany, Belgium and France. But it was not until 1921 that a free clinic was opened in South London where poor women could receive instruction in birth-control measures and medical attention and care. The credit for this belonged almost entirely to Dr. Marie Stopes, one of the pioneers and courageous champions of the movement.

It was not until 1914, however, that any organized attempt was made to circulate birth-control literature and educational information, following the arrest of Margaret Sanger for distributing her own pamphlet, *Family Limitation.* A registered nurse, Mrs. Sanger studied with Havelock Ellis in London and was associated with Dr. Stopes. In 1917, she organized the American Birth Control League and in 1921 started the first clinic in Brooklyn. This was promptly padlocked by the New York police and Mrs. Sanger was sentenced to thirty days in the workhouse; since 1873 it had been a federal offense to circulate birth-control information. Her conviction was appealed, however, and the Court of Appeals ruled that doctors could legally impart contraceptive data as a therapeutic measure. But it was not until 1923 that the first permanent birth-control clinic was established in New York City and was followed by similar institutions in other American communities.

From this it will be easy to see and understand why it was somewhat difficult, as well as dangerous, for a doctor to undertake any kind of open, aggressive campaign in behalf of the program back in 1907. For one thing, there really was no place for him to go in this country: there was no recognized organization in which he could be active; there were no clinics where he could give his professional services. As I have already pointed out, the entire movement had more the atmosphere of the Mafia or Camorra or a gang of Russian anarchists. This, to be sure, was through no fault or desire on the part of the birth-controllers themselves, but was forced on them by the harsh, stupid, repressive laws that made it a crime to disseminate knowledge.

But if I couldn't mount the barricades and join in the shooting war—as a matter of fact, I didn't even know where the "barricades" were located—I could and did make my small contribution in other, less spectacular ways, which were not altogether ineffective or without their uses. The war against ignorance, fear and superstition is a never-ending one; even more than courage, it requires patience and endurance. For nearly fifty years now, I have been working and fighting for the cause of birth control—not by making speeches, not by writing pamphlets, not by getting myself arrested—but by quietly and steadily advising, urging and pleading with my patients to exercise caution, if not restraint, and also by furnishing contraceptive information to all who need or want it. Naturally, I neither performed nor counseled illegal abortion, but whenever there were sound medical reasons for one I never hesitated to recommend it.

This, of course, frequently brought me into conflict with my Church and many devout laymen, including not a few of my Catholic colleagues. As much as it was in my power to do so, I avoided open, head-on collisions; but that was not always possible and on such occasions the atmosphere became charged with bitterness and anger. Sometimes it would take some weird, insane forms. One of my patients, a twenty-eight-year-old woman named Mrs. Hilda Harmon, became pregnant. Ordinarily, this would be cause for rejoicing, but in her case it was exactly the opposite, for she was suffering from cancer. Since pregnancy hastens the spread of the malignant cells throughout the body, it was obvious that the process of fertilization had to be reversed as speedily as possible. I sent her to the hospital at once and did a curettage on her, a surgical procedure of scraping the mucous membrane of the womb.

The operation is not especially difficult or dangerous, and Mrs. Harmon came out of it in excellent shape. Because of her general condition, however, I deemed it best for her to remain in the hospital for several days of rest and recuperation. One morning she had occasion to ring for a nurse in order to get some aspirin, or a bedpan, or something else to make her more comfortable. The nurse who answered happened to be a Catholic girl —let's call her Miss Donato—and she came to the patient's bedside wearing a black frown. When Mrs. Harmon asked her to do whatever it was she wanted done, Miss Donato shook her head and said, in effect, she wouldn't lift a finger to help her. When Mrs. Harmon wanted to know why, she explained that it would be a sin for her to aid a woman who had permitted an abortion to be performed on her. Mrs. Harmon protested that in the first place it had been medically necessary and was an entirely legal operation, no less than five doctors having testified it was essential to preserving her life. In the second place, Mrs. Harmon told her, she herself was not Catholic but Methodist, and it was not contrary to *her* religion. And finally, the hospital was not a Catholic one, but nonsectarian and a public institution.

These arguments made about as much impression on the nurse as a spitball would make on a rhinoceros. She still refused to assist her in any way; she wouldn't even touch her for fear of becoming "contaminated" by her "sin."

Naturally, Mrs. Harmon was rather stunned by this, to her, utterly un-Christian attitude. "You mean to say," she demanded, "if I were in serious danger, you would still not do anything to help me?" The nurse shook her head. Under no circumstances would she do anything for one who had been a party to killing an unborn child.

When my patient reported this to me it was more in a spirit of puzzled amusement than anger. To me, however, there was nothing amusing about it; I was thoroughly outraged and my first impulse was to have the girl fired immediately. Mrs. Harmon prevailed on me, though, not to ask for her dismissal, and I agreed not to. Nevertheless, it was my duty to report the incident officially to both the chief nurse and the superintendent. They could take whatever action they wished, but at least they should know that one of their nurses placed religious dogma above the oath she had taken to serve suffering humanity.

That the offender was forthwith discharged did not, however, in any way lessen my anger and fury at a blind doctrine that makes it possible for human beings to permit other human beings to suffer and even perish in the name of that gentle Saviour who died on the Cross to save mankind.

11 : Torna a Sorriento

THE GODS, IT IS SAID, are jealous of man's happiness, and perhaps I should have been warned that the contentment and peace which Elvira and I enjoyed could not last. Not that our years in America had been filled with unalloyed happiness; they had had more than their share of sorrows, of defeats and disappointments. But on the whole they had been a period of fruitful accomplishment and joyous fulfillment.

In March, 1908, a daughter was born to us whom we christened Minnie Filomena. A year and a half later, in September, 1909, Elvira gave birth to another child, this one a boy, and we gave him the same name as that of our firstborn, Joseph.

We were prospering in more material ways also. My practice had been building steadily, not only among my fellow Italian immigrants but among the wealthier, older native families—still because of the invisible influence of my "patroness," Madam Caroline. As a consequence, I was earning a fair amount of money each year—far more, indeed, than I had ever dreamed or hoped of earning—and I was able to salt away a rather sizable sum.

Doctors, like the majority of professional men, have demonstrated time and time again that as practical businessmen they are utterly inept. I was no exception.

By the end of 1909, when I had completed my third year

in the United States, I had succeeded in saving a little over $10,000. This was smoldering in my pocket, and I was not content to let it accumulate at compound interest in the savings bank. Nor was I minded to put it in government bonds or to invest in good common stocks, such as United States Steel or American Telephone & Telegraph, which, had I held on to them, would have made me a millionaire today. Like most Europeans, I had been conditioned to believe that land is the firm foundation of all wealth. This is no doubt sound economic doctrine, provided one really knows what he is doing and how to judge land values. Of course I knew nothing about real estate. I thought I did. From reading newspapers and talking to friends and patients who were in that field I acquired a smattering of knowledge which, I felt, fitted me to become an investor in Youngstown property. Of course, I did not realize it then, but I was suffering from the deadly disease of amateurism that has ruined and destroyed its thousands and its tens of thousands.

"Experience is the best of schoolmasters," declares Carlyle in one of his essays; "only the schoolfees are heavy." I paid a stiff fee to learn the limitations of the amateur in the real-estate business.

During 1909 I sank almost all my savings (and I use the word "sank" advisedly) in three houses in the Brier Hill section of Youngstown, which was its "Little Italy." My property was situated on one of the principal streets of that district and faced the railroad tracks. With typical lopsided amateur judgment, I had figured out that one day the railroad would want that land and I would turn a handsome profit. Here again I was the typical amateur, who generally plays by ear and depends on "hunches" and guesswork.

The outcome of my dabblings in real estate hardly needs to be told. It wouldn't be strictly accurate to say I lost my shirt, but I did lose all the buttons off of it plus a good-sized hunk of the tail. The railroad never enlarged its right-of-way and therefore never had any use for my property, which, simply as a piece of real estate, was of doubtful value because of the very fact that it was located alongside the tracks. The income it produced was small—not even sufficient to cover taxes and interest on the mortgage—and it grew smaller each year.

My purchase of real estate proved to be an unsound investment in another way, and one that was quite ironic, in view of the fact that it not only failed to yield me any return but cost me money. My professional colleagues and my fellow townsmen naturally discovered that I had assumed this new dignity of becoming a realty magnate. And human nature being what it is, they naturally took this as evidence of my success and became envious. Tongues began wagging, and I soon heard stories that I had got rich by charging exorbitant fees.

At this juncture, being considerably disturbed, I sought out one of my *paesani* from Agnone, Domenico Antonelli. More popularly known among the Italian community of Youngstown as Imbroglione, or Busybody, he was one of the numerous tribe of interpreters, at that time a fixture of every immigrant group in the United States. In reality, however, Imbroglione, like his confreres, was far more than merely an interpreter; he was a sort of liaison officer between Italian and non-Italian residents, a go-between, mediator, umpire, "honest broker" and general fixer-upper, an Americanized version of the Barber of Seville. He knew everyone in Brier Hill—Brianello, as it was Italianized—and everyone knew him. In fact, unofficially he was known as *il sindaco di Brianello,* the mayor of Brier Hill.

When I told him of the stories that were being circulated about me he nodded and said yes, he knew about them, indeed, had done his share of circulating. I told him I was shocked to know that he, one of my oldest, dearest friends in Youngstown, should believe and spread such a slander. He pulled down the outside corner of his right eyelid with one finger—a gesture in that eloquent sign language of southern Italy indicating profound and extreme skepticism—and shrugged. "Who said I *believe* it?"

"But if you do not," I said, "then how can you go about spreading such a story?"

"*Che differenza?*" he said. "What difference? Unless I repeat such tales people will think I am stupid, uninformed, no longer *in gamba*—on my toes."

"*Per Bacco!* By Bacchus!" I exclaimed. "Don't you see that you are helping to ruin me?"

He gave me a gentle, childlike smile and murmured, "*Piano, piano, caro dottore*—do not get yourself so excited. It is bad for the liver."

"Don't tell me what's good or bad for the liver! I know beter than you do, Imbroglione."

"Ah, yes, so you do! But about this silly business——"

"My reputation is not a 'silly business,' as you put it."

"No, of course not. But it was not to that I was referring, but to this stupid gossip——"

"If it's so stupid, then why do you help spread it?"

"I told you why. But that is not the important thing. The important thing is that you should not take it seriously."

"How can I help take it seriously?"

He placed his hand on my arm and explained that this was a normal occurrence not only in the Italian colony but in the Polish, Hungarian and German ones as well. Indeed, it was even a very healthy sign, for it meant that I had "arrived." Every foreign-born resident who had scored any sort of success in the United States had been subjected to the same kind of slander. As a matter of fact, according to Imbroglione, I ought to be glad people were saying such things about me.

"Maybe I should thank them?" I said.

"No, I don't think that is necessary," said he seriously. "But if I were you, *caro dottore,* I wouldn't worry about it too much. It won't last very long—that is, if you know how to meet it."

"And how does one go about meeting it?"

"By not meeting it at all. In other words, ignore it. Treat it with pride and with indifference, as if you did not know what people were saying. And if you can outlast them, then your position will be better than it ever was before."

At the time, it seemed more like counsel of despair, but time and events proved that Busybody was right. As the weeks passed

and I continued to keep up a bold bluff of not being concerned
with the slimy gossip and I made no attempt to fight it, the busy
tongues began to get tired of wagging and their owners bored,
and presently I started to notice a gradual upswing in my practice.

Imbroglione's advice is, of course, the only sound, intelligent
way to fight slander and scandal, as I have since discovered.
Against passive resistance and an unbreachable Chinese Wall of
silence it wears itself out and ultimately has to yield. A shrewd
politician once gave me his recipe for meeting attacks: wait at
least three days before counterattacking or uttering a word; if
at the end of that time the enemy is still attacking and the people
are paying attention to him, then it is time to answer; but in most
cases, if left alone, it will die by itself.

My acquisition of real estate did produce another and somewhat more melodramatic result, however. Just as the rumor-
mongering had about worn itself out I received an extortion
letter. I was ordered to place one thousand dollars in gold at a
certain lonely spot on the outskirts of town. I was warned that if
I failed to do so within the allotted time or informed the police,
I would pay with my life. In true movie style, the words were
spelled out with printed letters cut out of newspapers and magazines, and the signature consisted of the black silhouette of an
outspread hand.

At that period, the American press and public were as
aroused over the terroristic activities of the Mafia, or the Black
Hand, as they are today over Communists and juvenile delinquents. That there was, or may have been, much justification for
the popular hue and cry I do not doubt. Unquestionably the
Black Hand was responsible for many of the murders, kidnap-
pings and blackmailings that occurred during those years. But
it was my opinion then (and still is) that the threat was greatly
exaggerated and that many of the crimes that were charged up
against the Mafia were actually not perpetrated by its members
but by others who used its name for the double purpose of con-

cealing their own identity and terrorizing their victims more effectively.

I also believed that much of the Black Hand scare was stirred up not by Black Handers at all but rather by their supposed and loudly advertised "victims," who employed it as a means of obtaining publicity or, in some cases, as an excuse to avoid or delay paying their just debts. Or sometimes it was used to blacken and destroy the reputation of a business competitor, a political opponent or a rival in love. All one had to do was brand somebody a *manonerista,* a member of the Black Hand, and then the burden of proving he was *not* one rested on him—an exceedingly difficult, well-nigh impossible task. I had known three or four men who had been thus smeared, and I knew them to be honest, decent, hard-working, as capable of taking part in the activities of a secret terrorist organization as they were of becoming nuns. Yet each of them, to my own knowledge, was ruined.

I mention all this because it may help to explain why I did what I did. Instead of either reporting the extortion threat to the police or handing over a thousand dollars, I visited the spot indicated in the letter and left a letter of my own that read:

> I am not giving you any money now and I have no intention of giving you any in the future. I work much too hard for my money to hand it to any idiot who tries to frighten me with childish threats. If you really think you can kill me, try it and see what will happen. Good luck!

Every day for a whole week I went there and my note was still lying under the rock where I had been instructed to put the money. Finally on the eighth day it was gone. During the course of the next ten days, I received two more letters, containing still more dire threats. These I answered in the same fashion. Nothing happened, of course, and as the weeks went by I realized that my guess had been right, and they had merely been an attempt to bluff me out of money on the part of small-time crooks who lacked the nerve to follow through when their bluff was called.

The truth was, of course, that I was more lucky than smart, and it was only God's mercy that spared my loved ones and me much suffering and grief. I could and did crow about the happy outcome of my rashness. But putting it down on paper now, I feel rather ashamed of myself, and it is only my determination to be ruthlessly honest in setting out this record that causes me to relate the incident at all.

Nor (still being ruthlessly honest) did my folly end there, either. In my giddy bravado and confidence in my ability to out-bluff my would-be extortioners I made the mistake of telling Elvira about it. Not in the beginning, to be sure, but after my note had finally been collected and I got the first of the two follow-up letters. By that point I felt quite sure I was dealing with someone who was quite definitely not a Black Hander and who was probably not even a real professional in crime.

As I say, that was a mistake, a serious mistake. Being a physician, I should have known better. But even if I had not been a physician, I should have known that Elvira would worry and brood about it, would conjure up all sorts of unimaginable terrors, and when the danger was entirely past would suffer a severe letdown.

That was exactly what happened, and though she tried hard to conceal from me the source of her anxiety, it soon became apparent to me what had happened. Elvira had never been a particularly robust type. She had always been frail and weak, with a marked tendency to low blood pressure and anemia. Her three confinements had depleted her already none-too-abundant reserves of energy and strength. Moreover, she had never really become acclimated to North American weather, and the damp, foggy, smoke-laden atmosphere of Youngstown affected her not only physically but emotionally as well. She missed the clear, sparkling sunshine of our native mountain country, and the constant gray pall hanging over the Ohio city depressed and devitalized her mentally, in addition to causing her to suffer with increasing frequency from severe colds, grippe, influenza and various bronchial complaints, to the point where I began to worry about possible lung involvement. There had been, I remembered, a history of tuberculosis in her family, and while it is in no sense a hereditary disease, there was always the matter of susceptibility to be considered.

All this I had known for some time and had observed as it was developing, though I am quite certain she had no idea I had noticed the steady deterioration. But what I had not known and what I had not noticed until a short time after my brush with the extortioner was that she had also been suffering from a deep-seated, intense nostalgia. It was not only the bright sunlight and the clear air that she missed; it was Italy itself, and more especially Agnone and her family and all her childhood friends.

I knew Elvira well enough to know that she would drop in her tracks before she would utter a word of complaint to me; I decided the only way that anything was going to be done about it would be by my stepping in and taking charge. So one evening I sat down and had a talk with her and announced that I was sending her back to Italy with our children for a visit. She protested vehemently, of course. Her place was here, beside her husband. She refused to be separated from me, even for a day. And it simply was not true that she was unhappy in America. She had loved every day she had spent here. As for her health, well, perhaps she was a little tired and run down, but outside of that she was fine.

All of which I brushed aside. As her husband and physician I ordered her to return to Agnone. She continued to oppose it and finally, in order to get her to agree to it, I had to promise I would follow her there after a few months and bring her and the children back to the United States. So, on April 17, 1910, I took her and Minnie and Joseph to New York, and two days later they sailed for Europe. I returned to Youngstown, lonely and heavy of heart.

The weeks and months that passed were empty, bitter ones for me. Never in my entire existence had I been so miserable. Several times I was almost on the point of chucking everything and going to Italy myself, and I might have done so, had there been anyone around who could have taken over my practice for a few months. But since there was no one I had to stick it out.

Then I toyed with the idea of trying to sell my practice altogether and getting rid of my real estate, even though that would mean taking a sizable loss on it. What I had in the back of my mind was to go to Paris and do some work at the Sorbonne under one of the most eminent dermatologists in Europe. After a couple of years of study I would return to the States to specialize in that branch of medicine. But not in Youngstown, in some much larger city—Cleveland, or Chicago, or even New York. Now I knew I did not have to depend on my fellow Italian immigrants to succeed. My English had improved considerably during the nearly four years I had been living in the United States. I hadn't entirely lost my accent, it's true, but that would enhance rather than lessen my chances in a specialty, for that was still the era when most Americans regarded European-trained specialists superior to their own.

The truth was, of course, that the real cause of my desire to return to Europe was not further study or even Elvira and the children; it was my boredom and restlessness, my gypsy love of adventure that was stirring me up again. The old urge to be on the move once more was boiling up within me; I sought new challenges to meet and conquer.

One afternoon in the following November I was hurrying to an emergency call. Since it was quite near my office I walked, figuring it would take less time than starting my car, driving and having to park it. (Even in 1910 that was already a problem.) There had been an early snowfall a couple of days before—"How nice!" everybody had said. "Just in time for Thanksgiving!"— and the streets were quite slippery. I dashed along, my mind fixed on some distant horizon. Suddenly as I started to cross Federal Avenue, I heard a noise. I glanced up. An auto was bearing straight down on me. I pullled back sharply and my feet slid out from under me. Then I felt the car hitting me and everything went black.

When I came to I found myself in exactly the same place I had been expecting to send my patient—the hospital. My left arm and leg were swathed in bandages; the entire left side of my body seemed to be one enormous ache. But my first panicky thought was that my leg and arm had been fractured, or worse.

There was a nurse, an excellent one whom I had used on many of my cases, a Miss Richards, sitting in the room near my bed. Fearfully, I asked her how seriously I had been injured. She smiled and assured me no major damage had been done, no bones broken, no ribs cracked, no muscles or ligaments torn. I had been very lucky, she said. The auto had been traveling slowly, for one thing; and my slipping had twisted my body around so that the full force of the blow was deflected.

All told, my accident kept me in the hospital for a full week. The nervous shock and the inevitable emotional letdown that follows such a trauma, however, plagued me for weeks afterward. Then the combination of that, overwork, worry and indigestion from eating in restaurants all the time, now that I had become a grass widower, caused my entire digestive apparatus to go out of commission. By the time spring finally rolled around I was licked.

But there was still just enough of the instinct of self-preservation left in me to make one last, desperate attempt to save myself. After considerable inner turmoil and debate I at last decided to prescribe for myself the same remedy I had prescribed for my very first "bootleg" patient in America—a good stiff dose of my own "native mountain air." I would return to Agnone, spend four, five, six months there, as long as might be necessary to bring my physical, mental, emotional and spiritual "tone" back to normal. Then I would determine what my next step would be, whether to go to Paris, return to the States, remain in Italy or whatever. By then, too, Elvira would be also recovered and could accompany me wherever we both decided to go, for this time I would consult her wishes as well as my own.

In accordance with this plan, I decided to sell both my practice and my property in Youngstown. The practice I had little trouble disposing of at a good price to a young but very capable American doctor. The property, however, was quite a different story. Perhaps if I had had more energy and strength, and if I had been less eager to return to Italy in a hurry, I might have succeeded in getting rid of it. As it was, unless I was prepared to sell it for less than a quarter of what I paid for it, I had to continue to hold it, and I placed the management of it in the hands of an agent with instructions to find a buyer, if that was at all possible.

On the evening of June 8, 1911, I boarded a Pennsylvania train for New York. The next day, at high noon, I sailed for Italy on the *Oceania*. It was five and a half years, almost to the day, since I had first set foot on American soil with Elvira by my side. As I leaned against the ship's rail and watched the serene goddess of liberty fade into the distance I wondered, what have all these months and years, since that cold, gray December day, what have they really added up to in the great ledger of life? To success? To failure? To happiness? To lasting, meaningful accomplishment? Had I moved forward? Backward? Or merely stood still?

It was quite true that I was going back to where I had started. Some might construe this as defeat, as a retreat. Yet, by being as honest with myself as I could, it did not seem so to me. After all, I had gone off on my great adventure. I had met the challenge of a strange, new country. I had succeeded in establishing myself in my profession as well as in the community I had chosen to live and work in. I had built up a thriving medical practice— not the richest, by any means, but certainly a comfortable one— and I had earned the respect of my fellow practitioners and the confidence of my patients. I had also won a place of some honor and dignity in the life of the community, a not-too-negligible achievement for one who had come to these shores only a few years before as a stranger scarcely able to speak the language of its people. I had made a home for my wife and had established a family. And I was returning to the land of my birth far richer in worldly goods than when I had left it.

But the one thing that I regarded as my most important and most gratifying accomplishment was none of these. It was quite simply this: I was going back to Italy not as an Italian, or even as an ex-Italian, but as an American. That, to me, was my proudest achievement.

As I gazed down at the green water performing its lacy ballet along the ship's side I pondered the ancient sphinx riddle, asking myself that question that is as old as man himself, that Adam must have asked himself as he strode from the Garden of Eden: *What does the future hold for me now?*

PART TWO

In the midway of this our mortal life,
I found me in a gloomy wood astray,
Gone from the path direct.
—DANTE

12: Return of the Non-Prodigal Son

THE SAME FEARS, the same doubts and misgivings that had
gnawed at me as I was about to set foot in the United States,
assailed me now as I prepared to step onto Italian soil once more.
For twenty-five years I had called this land my home: emotionally, spiritually, it had been the only home I had ever known.
But now, as I was approaching it, I felt like a stranger entering
a strange land. I told myself it hadn't changed; it couldn't; it was
the same now as it had been five and a half years before and as
it had been for centuries before that. Italy is an eternally magnificent woman whose mature beauty can never fade or perish.
"Things do not change," Thoreau declares; "we change." The
word *Italy* that had once been "graved inside" my heart had
been erased and another written in its place—*America*.

Even the sight of Vesuvius, sporting its white plume of
smoke like Cyrano's proud panache, failed to stir within me the
thrill of homecoming. On the contrary, it aroused an emotion
very similar to the one I had felt that bleak December day when
first I looked upon the Statue of Liberty. Instead of being flooded
with joy and anticipation, my heart was heavy, my spirit weighed
down by nameless forebodings and dark self-questionings.

Before we landed at Naples we learned that an outbreak of
cholera was raging in and around the city. The day prior to our
arrival no fewer than eighty-seven new cases had been reported

and nineteen deaths. I needed no one to warn me of the dangers of epidemic cholera morbus. As soon as I debarked from the *Oceania* I took a cab and rushed to the railroad station and took the first train to the railhead at Carovilli, some ten miles west of Agnone, wiring Elvira to meet me there with our children.

After more than a year's separation our reunion bordered on the hysterical. What was said and done is scarcely important, even were it possible to recall. The only thing that mattered was that we were together again and, God willing, we would remain together for a long, long time to come.

The trip from Carovilli to Agnone was by stagecoach, and the moment I laid eyes on that rickety, antique vehicle and heard the silver bells tinkling around the horses' necks a strange and wonderful peace descended upon me. Their music carried me back to the past, to childhood, to those high, lyric days of my first awakening love for Elvira, now sitting by my side. And as we rolled and rocked along the narrow, bumpy, dusty roads twisting through the green-robed foothills, past the fields of unripened wheat and the olive groves gleaming in the hot sun, past the miles of neat hedges splashed with poppies, daisies, irises, wild roses and tiger lilies, past the Verrino weaving through the tapestry of brown and green like a pale, golden thread, I found myself growing more and more relaxed and calm and untroubled. For the first time in many, many weeks— indeed in many months—I began to feel a deep contentment, a sense of again belonging, of reaching a terminal point where I would find rest and refreshment of the spirit as well as of the body. Now all the old, familiar sights, and sounds, and smells came pouring back, as if the dikes of conscious thought had been breached and a tidal wave of memories had come rushing through. The singing of the birds, the bittersweet piping of an invisible shepherd's reed, the tolling of distant bells, the sad song of a girl walking along the road . . . how tender, how melancholy, how hauntingly beautiful they were, and each in turn, or in unison, or alone, or in counterpoint, chanted the same happy refrain into my innermost, secret ear . . . *You are coming home! you are coming home! coming, coming, coming home!*

Then suddenly—I had almost forgotten it—we swung around the shoulder of a hill and there, across the narrow valley, perched on the edge of her plateau, there was Agnone, her fourteen church steeples gleaming above her houses ascending in white waves crested with pink, seeming more like some tiny toy town fashioned by a child than a real community in which dwelled flesh-and-blood men and women. And as I gazed at it through a haze of dust and sun I felt my eyes get heavy and hot, and the view became blurred. I knew then that I was home.

The welcome I received at the hands of my fellow townsmen, my *cittadini,* would have more than satisfied the biblical prodigal son. For a while it seemed as if the round of monumental dinners, parties, balls and other festivities, for which my return provided a more than adequate excuse, would never end. In between these celebrations and the more or less regular, routine social activities—the birthdays, baptisms, weddings, communions, each of which had to be marked by a *festa*—I managed to squeeze in some of the hardest, most concentrated and serious resting of my entire existence. During those first months following my return I became the greatest exponent of *dolce far niente* in all Italy. I followed Whitman's famous precept with literal faithfulness and I, too, could truthfully proclaim:

> I loaf and invite my soul,
> I lean and loaf at my ease observing a spear of summer grass.

In addition to making observations on the summer grass, I also did a considerable amount of reading, some hunting and fishing, and took long, leisurely strolls through the woods. My old friend and colleague, Dr. Luigi Cremonese, took off for a midsummer vacation, and he tried to persuade me to look after his practice for him while he was away, but I was far too busy inviting my soul and enjoying the first real rest I had had in a dozen years or more. This was what *my* physician had prescribed, and I was going to be a model patient.

Life, however, is actually little more than a series of teasing ironies and paradoxes; what I had refused to do for good, hard cash I soon found myself doing out of sentiment and sympathy.

Though I had let it be known far and wide that I had not come back to practice, that I was *molto in vacanza,* very much on a holiday, and that I would not even look at a sick person, let alone treat him, still the lame, the halt and the blind came knocking on my door. This was not only very flattering but touching as well, especially since almost all of those who sought me out were hopeless cases who had been given up by every doctor in the vicinity and who, in turn, had given up every doctor. I would have needed a heart made of armor plate and filled with ice water to turn away their simple faith in the wonder-working abilities of *l'Americano* and his miraculous "mouse-trap."

The first of these patients was a twenty-three-year-old girl suffering from an active pulmonary tuberculosis. It was far advanced, and it required no profound knowledge of medicine or any great diagnostic insight to tell that she was not very long for this world. But she looked at me with her fever-bright black eyes, shining out of shadowed pits sunk deep in her dead-white, shrunken face, and told me that her brother had written her about all the marvels that were daily being wrought by God and the Americans. It only seemed logical, then, that I, who had spent six years among them, should also be able to work medical prodigies, such as healing weak lungs.

To tell this poor girl the truth would have been worse than cruel; it would have been pointless. All that any earthly physician could possibly do for her was to attempt to ease the agony and lessen the mental anguish that must usher her out of this life. Since I could hardly prescribe "native mountain air" for her, I did the next best thing. I gave her a placebo, a foul-tasting tonic with a label printed in English and the name and address of a Youngstown pharmacist. Aside from its flavor and odor it was quite harmless, but the mere fact of its having come from America and being horrible to take removed any and all doubts as to its miracle-producing properties. She accepted it eagerly and gulped down a generous slug straight from the bottle. I couldn't help wincing, but fortunately she did not notice it.

"I knew you would save me, Doctor!" she exclaimed, tears of

joy glistening in her eyes. "You have saved me! I knew you would! I knew it! Ah, *grazie, grazie!*" She fell to her knees, seized my hand and kissed it a dozen times or more in a rapture of gratitude. I lifted her gently to her feet.

Now she embarrassed me still more by trying to force a five-lira piece on me in payment for my services. This was not a tremendous sum of money, of course—at that time it was the equivalent of an American dollar—but for her, as for most of her countrymen, it represented a good deal of hard work, perhaps two or three days of labor in the fields or orchards.

Naturally, I refused to take her money. She argued with me, she pleaded and cajoled, she stormed and cried, and for a moment I feared she was going to drop to her knees again and cover my hands with her kisses. Finally, though, when she realized I wasn't going to budge, she tried to get me to accept payment "in kind"—some fruit, or vegetables, or cheese—and when I refused that also she wanted to know how she could repay me for my kindness and help.

"Just get well," I said.

But recovery was the one thing she could never give me. I like to think that my auto-suggestive therapy may have served to prolong the flickering candle of her life a little longer and to make her last days on earth a trifle brighter. But auto-suggestion, as I knew, alas, too well, is no cure for tuberculosis, and when the cold, brown fingers of autumn began to fondle the trees she slipped away, like the girl in O. Henry's famous story, with the first falling leaves.

A few days later a peasant couple came to see me. The woman carried a boy of about three in her arms, and the father lugged a bulky cradle fashioned out of twigs with a torn straw mattress and a ragged, faded shred of blanket in it. Their child had an enormously swollen head, but his face and limbs were shrunken. His history had been swelling of the cranium that had started when he was about one month old, and shortly afterward he had begun to have epileptic seizures. He had never walked or talked or made any sound other than a feeble moan or cry. His parents had spent every penny they possessed and had borrowed more to pay doctors for draining water from his skull and spine; they had even been lured into buying some sort of contraption to perform the same futile operation mechanically.

The boy was afflicted with chronic hydrocephalus—in layman's language, "water on the brain"—which consists of fluid accumulating in the membranes and the lateral ventricles of the brain, the cavities along each side of the skull. As the amount of liquid increases the ventricles become distended; that causes the upper portion of the head to expand abnormally. Since the disease most frequently occurs during the first six months of life when the cranial bones have not yet fused together, an enormous amount of expansion can take place before any actual destructive pressure is put on the brain. Ultimately, however, the cerebral functions become impaired and the child's mental powers damaged, particularly his senses of sight and hearing. The victim generally develops marked symptoms of listlessness, irritability and apathy, and in many cases becomes completely imbecilic. The prognosis is almost invariably hopeless, though in a very few, rare instances hydrocephalitics have been known to live on into old age. In the vast majority, however, the life expectancy is extremely low—mercifully so for all concerned.

I knew that the child was doomed and I wondered at my colleagues who had attempted to treat him. The parents, of course, had come to me in the same spirit as the girl with T.B.—because I had just returned from America, where miracles are performed while you wait. They were certain I possessed some special magic that would work where all the local medicine men had failed. Thus it became my painful, unpleasant duty to break the dreadful truth to them. It was one thing, I felt, to deceive a poor wisp of a girl in order to make her final days of suffering a little more endurable; it was quite another, however, to delude a mother and father and not to prepare them for the inevitable. I tried to make them understand that it would be God's mercy for that to happen, and quickly.

They listened to me in silence, stunned, incredulous. For a

second, I thought they hadn't comprehended what I told them. Then the mother broke into a spasm of the most unearthly sobbing I ever heard. It made me shiver. It didn't seem to come from inside her frail body, but from somewhere below her, deep in the earth. And through all this keening she kept kissing the baby's lips. Somehow, despite all my sympathy, I couldn't help thinking of Salome and John the Baptist, and shuddering. As for the husband, he just stood there, looking at his wife in stupefied, stoical silence. After several minutes, however, she began to grow calmer and the man tenderly lifted the child out of her arms and placed him in the cradle, covering him with that wretched patch of blanket.

"*Grazie, mille grazie, signor dottore,*" he said. "A thousand thanks, Doctor."

"*E niente,*" I said. "Nothing at all.

He, too, tried to pay me. He apologized because they could not give me any money—the other doctors had taken all their *denaro*—but they would gladly give me a couple of chickens or a suckling pig. Again I refused, and they were too numbed and grief-stricken to protest.

I asked them what they were going to do now and the man replied, "We go to no more doctors. *Basta!* Enough! If you who have come from America cannot help our Peppino, then there is only one other who can save him."

"And who is that?" I asked, wondering whether they had some final wonder-working physician in reserve.

They did. But he was no doctor of medicine. "We will take our little one to St. Donatus. He will make him well. Forever blessèd be his name!" The father crossed himself, then touched the floor with his fingertips and kissed them. I would not, I could not, argue against that. Certainly no earthly medicine could cure the *bambino*. Maybe faith, which was supposed to be able to move mountains, could accomplish the unaccomplishable.

They left. At a discreet distance I followed them. Frankly, I was a bit curious to observe what my saintly colleague might do for the boy. There is a tiny church a couple of kilometers out-

side Agnone in which stood a statue of San Donato that was said
to have miraculous powers, particularly in healing children who
were lame and crippled or had some speech defect. In return
for his intercession it was customary to offer him corn, wheat,
olives, fruit or some other form of produce. On the way to the
shrine the couple stopped at a small, run-down farm, presumably
their own, and the man disappeared inside the barn. A few
moments later he came out, an immense sack stuffed with grain
on his back.

At the church he deposited the sack by the door. Then he
took the baby in his arms. The woman immediately dropped to
her knees, and remaining in that position, she proceeded to draw
a line with her tongue down the entire length of the nave from
just inside the door to the altar, where stood the wonder-working
figure of the saint carved in alabaster of golden translucence. The
distance must have been a good 150 feet, at least, and by the
time she had reached the altar rail her tongue was a raw, filthy,
bleeding pulp. She crossed herself again and through her bloody
lips and swollen tongue she implored the saint for *grazia e pietà*,
grace and mercy, for her son, then burst into another paroxysm
of blood-chilling sobs and groans as though she were suddenly
possessed.

Garbed in gorgeous, gold-encrusted vestments, the priest knelt
before the altar, the white-robed sacristan beside him, two altar
boys solemnly swinging their censers. They prayed throughout
the woman's frenzied ravings, and when at last she had become
quiet, they rose, nodded to her and her husband and marched
into the sacristy. The woman took the child back in her arms; the
man collected his sack, and they followed the others into the
sacristy, which was now crowded with worshippers grouped about
an immense silver scale.

While the priest prayed sonorously the father placed his child
in one pan of the scale and the sack in the other, while the sacristan held both of them level.

"*Chiudete gli occhi!*" the sacristan barked. "Close your eyes!"
The faithful snapped their eyelids together, though I suspect

most of them, like me, left just a sliver open so that they could see what was going on. A mumble of prayer filled the chamber as they joined the priest in his devotions.

At the end of perhaps three minutes the priest intoned, "Amen," and without a second's pause whipped out the command, *"Lasci'andar la bilancia!* Let go of the scales!"

That was our cue to open our eyes, and as we did so the sacristan released his grip on the scale and the pan with the grain on it dipped sharply and the other, containing the boy, rose proportionately. The crowd emitted a collective exclamation of surprise and joy. The husband and wife embraced, then snatched up their son and began kissing him excitedly.

"Deo gratias!" the priest chanted. He made the sign of the cross upon the crowd. *Laus Deo! Laus Deo!"* He nodded to the sacristan to gather in the grain and disappeared, the sacristan staggering after him under his heavy load.

As the weeks lengthened into months and more and more people beat a path to the Americano's wonder-working "mouse-trap," I found myself growing increasingly restless. Nature had healed my tired body and soothed my spirit. Further rest and idleness would mean only irritation. I was eager to return to my normal, busy, active way of life, to become a full-time practicing physician once more. I began thinking of returning to the States, consulting the sailing schedules, debating with myself whether to go straight back to America at once or to follow through on my interrupted plan of studying dermatology in Paris.

I made the mistake of reckoning without Dame Circumstance, who proceeded now with what seemed to me to be methodical malice to derail and wreck my schemes. First of all, early in the summer of 1913 Elvira bore me another son. Since he was born in Italy, we named him Italo.

The arrival of a third child had an incidental effect on me; it began to infect me with delusions of grandeur. Now that the Lord had blessed me with two fine sons and a daughter I felt that the "house" of the Daniele must once again be placed on a firm, enduring foundation. Nothing would do but a magnificent *palazzo* that would be worthy of our ancient and honored family. I had been able to purchase back our old house, and proceeded to have it demolished and to erect a splendid mansion on its site. This took almost every dollar I had accumulated in the United States, and when it was completed I had a truly regal residence that could have been and should have been named "Daniele's Folly." Even had I intended to remain in Italy and to occupy my stately mansion I would have had great difficulty maintaining such a princely establishment; for it required at the very minimum three servants, and the taxes, even for Italy, were a far from inconsiderable item. But my idea had been to rent it while I lived in America, keeping it in my possession as a sort of official "family seat" and one day, perhaps, after I had made my fortune in the States to use it for summer or winter visits.

This grandiose plan quickly met the fate it deserved. I soon discovered that although many Agnonesi would have liked living in the new Palazzo Daniele, none could afford to pay what I had to ask for rent. Nor could I sell it, without taking a terrific loss. The difference between a wise man and a fool, I was once told, is that while both make mistakes, the fool keeps making the same mistakes in the same way and the wise man makes them in a different way. By that definition I surely qualified as a fool. After my sorry experience in Youngstown as a real-estate holder I should have learned my lesson, but apparently I hadn't.

On top of this fiasco I suffered another blow. During September my mother had had a severe paralytic stroke. This, naturally, occupied much of my time and attention, even though I had another physician attend her; and it caused me great anxiety. She made a gallant, determined fight against it and was making slow, steady progress all through that autumn and winter. But early in February, 1914, she suffered another, even more violent stroke and two days later she died.

Now the winter of my discontent really closed in upon me. Agnone and Italy itself depressed me. I had exhausted all their charms and all their delights. I had had my fill. But I made another fatal error. I hesitated, I lingered too long. My timing was bad.

While I debated whether to go straight back to America or to detour via Paris and the Sorbonne; while I delayed my departure until I could find a tenant or a purchaser for my *palazzo;* while I tried to decide whether I desired to specialize in dermatology or to continue in general practice . . . great and terrible events were taking shape. By now winter had fled, spring was almost over, and the first hot breath of summer had heralded the coming of a new season. May slipped past and June was nearly gone. Then, on June 28, a scant two hundred and fifty miles straight across the Adriatic Sea, a series of pistol shots rang out in an obscure, unpronounceable city named Sarajevo in an obscure, un-pronounceable province named Bosnia-Herzegovina. Like nearly everyone else, I dismissed it as merely another foolish flurry in the Balkans, that perennial inflammation on the face of Europe. There would be the usual brisk volleying of diplomatic notes be-tween the various capitals. The German Kaiser would perform his customary saber-rattling ritual; the Russian bear would emit a few menacing growls; France would inflict a few deft pinpricks on the Teutonic rump; the Austrian emperor would call upon his personal ally, the Holy Ghost, to destroy their common enemies; and England, carefully teetering on her balance of power, would do absolutely nothing, and do it exceedingly well. Then, after this international minuet was over and Austrian "honor" had been avenged, everyone would gracefully and gratefully return to the familiar *status quo ante* and wait for the next dance. After all, no one was interested in fighting a war merely because an un-popular and rather disagreeable Austrian archduke and his social-climbing, parvenu duchess happened to get themselves assassi-nated.

That was the way I saw it that sunny, serene morning of June 29, 1914. If I misread the omens like a blind fool, at least I had the dubious comfort of knowing I had the company of countless millions of other fools all over the globe—including,

I'm sure, the emperors of Germany and Austria, the czar of Russia, the king of Italy and the rulers of France and Britain.

So I blithely went ahead with my plans and preparations for returning to the United States with Elvira and our children in mid-September. But my timing was bad. By the third week of July the sands of easy optimism began to run out swiftly. On the twenty-third Austria issued her ultimatum to Serbia and five days later, one month to the day after the death of Archduke Franz Ferdinand, Austrian forces crossed the frontier into Serbia. Within a week the first World War had engulfed Europe.

Although a member of the Triple Alliance, Italy was obligated to go to the aid of her allies, Germany and Austria, only in the event of their being attacked. Inasmuch as they were the attackers, not the attacked, Italy was absolved from entering the conflict on their side. This news naturally gladdened my heart, for I felt it would still be possible for us to return to America. But I was speedily disillusioned. The Italian government issued a decree "freezing" all doctors under the age of thirty-seven. They would not be permitted to leave the country until further notice. Since I was thirty-five I found myself among the frozen. Shortly thereafter I was asked if I would volunteer to serve in the Royal Army Medical Corps, should Italy decide to enter the war. Since this seemed to be the clear path of duty and since, more important, it didn't appear likely that I should be able to leave the country for a long time to come, I agreed to serve when and if such an emergency arose. I didn't honestly know why I did it, nor did I know whom we would be fighting.

But one thing I did know, and that only too, too well—I was trapped.

13 : I Am Offered the Key
to a Bordello

SINCE I COULD NOT PRACTICE medicine in the United States, at least for a while, I would practice it in Italy. It would be, as the French say, *faute de mieux,* but anything was preferable to the tedium of a life of leisure. Fortunately for me, I was offered the post of municipal doctor in the small town of Cingoli, in the province of Marche, just above my native province of Abruzzi-Molise.

It should be understood that for quite a considerable period in Italy we had had what might be termed socialized medicine. Local municipalities would have assigned to them one or more practitioners whose duty it was to treat any and all citizens of the community without charge, the townspeople paying for their services out of taxes, the doctors receiving fixed weekly stipends. In addition, each municipality maintained one or more combination dispensaries and ten- to fifty-bed infirmaries, the larger towns having full-size hospitals.

On March 15, I left for Cingoli. Over her rather violent protests, I made Elvira remain in Agnone with the children. I had two reasons for doing this. First, my appointment was only a temporary one. Second, by that time there was much talk about Italy getting into the war after all, and if that happened, I would immediately be called into the Army. It seemed foolish, therefore, for Elvira to break up our home in Agnone to move to a tiny rural town and get settled there, only to have to move again in maybe four, five, eight months—or even in a matter of weeks.

Cingoli is about twenty-five miles west of Ancona, Italy's principal Adriatic port between Bari in the South and Venice in the North. I took the train to Ancona and from there a stage-coach.

When I arrived in the main—and only—piazza of the town, I found a reception committee on hand to greet me and to look me over. I caught a number of comments from people in the crowd, none of which especially gladdened my soul. "He's a shrimp, like the other one," a man said. "Not too bad-looking," a woman remarked. And another man growled, "Hope he knows his business better than that other butcher we had!"

The leader of the welcoming group was a large, florid man in black clerical garb. He was a handsome, impressive figure with the cool green eyes of an eagle and a nose that would have done credit to the same bird. Nevertheless, in spite of his stern appearance he proved to be a most amiable and warmhearted soul. Besides being the town's only spiritual leader, Don Nicola was also secretary of the municipal council, and it was in this capacity that he was now serving. When he learned that my *signora* was remaining in Agnone, he graciously invited me to stay in his home, and in order to dispel any fears I might have that this was merely a courteous but empty gesture, he quickly added that it was customary for all the wifeless municipal doctors to be "quartered" with him.

Including Cingoli's civic leaders, all three of them, and a miscellaneous crowd of well-wishers, idlers and children, an informal procession escorted Don Nicola and me to his *casa* through the narrow, twisting streets and alleys. As we marched along I couldn't help thinking back to that December day more than eight years before, and a similar welcoming committee in Youngstown. Similar, yet so different.

Don Nicola had arranged an official "state dinner" that evening in my honor. To it were invited all the leading citizens of Cingoli, including, naturally, *il sindaco,* the mayor; the sole schoolteacher, who was a girl of perhaps twenty-eight or twenty-nine; the commander of the local *carabinièri* detachment; several of the important businessmen; Donna Letizia and Don Attilio, our host's sister and diminutive brother-in-law; and Don Andrea, an immense priest who was Don Nicola's assistant.

The dinner, like all such Italian rituals, was delicious, rich, stupefying, and took forever to serve and eat and even longer to get over. The only thing that stands out in my memory about it was one particular topic that came up during the course of our table talk. As it happened, it was a Friday and I was somewhat surprised to see Don Andrea eating boiled chicken in place of the fish the rest of us were having. It was difficult to understand how a Catholic priest could violate, openly and unashamed, one of the cardinal rules of the Church's dogma.

"Ahimè! I am a slave to my stomach," he said sighing between bites of the plump, tender chicken leg. "My stomach is extremely delicate. It refuses any food that is the least bit coarse. This is the only thing it will accept. Alas! What can I do? It is God's will that I be condemned to eat chicken every day." With that he crossed himself and his eyes turned heavenward, looking like a pair of unpeeled eggs.

This caused the pharmacist to raise the question that perhaps Don Andrea's evacuation was faulty and what he needed was a good course of purgatives. This, in turn, set off an animated, even rather heated debate as to the importance of regularity in bowel movements, what periods of the day were best to have them, the advantages and disadvantages of cathartics, suppositories and enemas, with learned Latin quotations bombarding both sides. Oddly enough, although I was the only person at the table with any real knowledge and experience in medical matters, no one bothered to consult my opinion, and I was careful to keep out of the discussion. Finally, however, the schoolteacher couldn't stand any more of this extremely candid, clinical conversation, and she jumped up and bolted out of the room.

The next morning I woke early. I went out onto the balcony that overlooked the countryside. The sun, newly risen above the horizon, was a brilliant vermilion ball suspended in an arching sky that shaded from pale blue to indigo. Before and below me stretched a billowing panorama of rolling hills and valleys clothed in their fresh apple-green spring finery on which were embroidered clusters of white, red, pink and yellow houses. Far in the distance, gleaming in the coppery rays of the ascendant sun, I could make out the delicately tinted turquoise of the Adriatic. The air was pungent with the smell of pine, but subtly softened with the scent of the budding blossoms of the orange and lemon groves nestling in the valleys.

My reverie was interrupted by the provocative aroma of strong black coffee and the voice of Filomena, Don Nicola's cook, booming out a lusty *"Buon giorno, signor dottore!"* She was carrying a cup of steaming coffee for me, and as I sipped it she gazed at the view admiringly for a moment or two, then asked me how I liked Cingoli. I said I thought it was very lovely indeed. She wanted to know how Italy compared with America, and I told her America was a wonderful country too, but in a different way; there life was more intense, swifter, fiercer; the rewards were greater, but the costs of winning them much greater also.

She listened to me closely, nodding her head. When I had concluded she remained silent for a second; then her fine, large blue eyes seemed to soften and she came forth with a remark that was quite startling. "America," she said, "the Lord made on a beautiful day. Europe, He made in a dark night." Frankly, at the time, I didn't quite know what it meant. I still don't, for that matter, but it seemed a striking thought and one that must be pregnant with meaning.

Later that morning, as Don Nicola, his sister and brother-in-law and I were finishing breakfast, three visitors were announced —to see me, not my host. One was a good-looking young fellow called Gigetto with a great mop of light blond hair that gave his head the appearance of a roof thatched with straw. He was a coachman and his only job was working for the municipality, providing transportation for the city physician. As I later learned, he got paid only by the trip, and if the doctor made no outside calls, Gigetto didn't get paid. That made things rather difficult for him, because he not only had a wife and three small children but also a blind father and a crippled mother who were dependent on him.

His two companions, a man and a woman, ran the local infirmary. Gennaro was a short, wiry midget of a man with an oversized jet-black beard and mustache which, combined with his too-brisk, too-bustling manner, gave the impression of a slightly delirious monkey. This was still further strengthened by his tiny pale-brown eyes that darted glances in all directions like a couple of jumping beans. The woman with him was his wife, Custode, and she was a trained nurse (he said) and assisted him in taking care of patients admitted to the infirmary.

According to Gennaro, the previous incumbent of my high office left the couple to run things pretty much by themselves and did not bother with treating patients himself except in cases of extreme illness. Naturally this struck me as a rather astonishing state of affairs, but I refrained from making any comment at that time, deciding that patience would be the better part of wisdom. I let Gennaro run on, for by listening one always learns.

And what I learned perplexed and disturbed me. Apparently my predecessor had given the couple complete authority and had exercised little or no supervision over them. This might have been all right had they been well trained and experienced, but I had an uneasy feeling, merely from the way they spoke, that they had very little knowledge of medicine, if any at all.

"Custode and I are most efficient," Gennaro assured me. "Dr. Papini trusted us completely."

"Yes, I'm sure of that," I said noncommittally.

"If you're planning to spend more time at the infirmary than he did, Doctor," he said, "I am sure *we* can work together."

The insolence of that statement made me bristle, and it was only by dint of great self-control that I was able to keep from losing my temper. But I somehow managed to remain calm. In no uncertain terms I made it clear that I intended to visit the infirmary regularly, and that I would examine and prescribe for all patients who would be admitted there, and that I would hold Gennaro and his wife accountable for carrying out my orders to the letter and if they failed to . . .

I purposely left the thought unfinished, or at least unvoiced; I was certain Gennaro and Custode knew what I meant and what would happen to them should they decide to mutiny. If I had any doubts as to their understanding my intentions, they were dispelled by Gennaro himself. For he frowned worriedly and shrugged, as if to say, *Well, if you wish to be an unreasonable fool and alienate us, we can't stop you. But don't look to us for help.*

This telepathic message I ignored. Instead, in a quiet but firm tone I said, "As for working together, I take it for granted at all times that my associates and I will work together. And I am sure," I added with a somewhat mocking smile, "that you and your wife *will* work together with me."

He and Custode started to protest their undying loyalty and devotion, but I cut them short by demanding to know how many patients were in the infirmary at the moment. Only one, they told me; a nineteen-year-old girl had come in the previous day with a bad wound on her forehead. Gennaro had put nine stitches in it and he proposed to remove them that very afternoon at four o'clock. I asked him why he hadn't summoned me the day before (the girl had come in several hours after my arrival in Cingoli), and he shrugged again, said something about not having wanted to disturb me only a few hours after my getting there; after all, it was nothing very serious, just a superficial flesh wound.

"Don't you realize that no head wound is trivial or superficial, Gennaro?" I said. "Not until the possibility of a skull fracture or concussion has been ruled out. Surely you won't pretend to be able to diagnose head injuries? By the way, how *did* she get injured?"

"*Non lo so, signor dottore,*" he said, "I don't know, Doctor. She says she was cleaning a closet and a bottle fell out and struck her forehead." His shrug eloquently expressed his unspoken doubts.

"Who is the girl?" said Don Nicola.

"Dorotea Alda."

"Arturo's daughter?"

"*Sì.*"

"Doesn't he work for the *marchese?*" asked Don Attilio.

"*Sì.*"

That rather puzzled me. I knew that this infirmary, like all other municipal infirmaries, was intended only for the poor who could not afford to pay for doctor, medication and hospital care. What was the daughter of a man who worked for the immensely rich Marquess of San Costanza doing in a public infirmary?

Gennaro explained that though not only her father was employed by the *marchese,* but her mother, her three brothers, four sisters and herself also, nevertheless they were quite poor. Besides, emergency accident cases could be handled in the infirmary no matter what the economic circumstances might or might not be.

I could sense—indeed, I could *see*—that Gennaro was quite uncomfortable as he explained how and why Dorotea's family were not well off. It was obvious that there was much more he might have told me and would have liked to tell me, but didn't care or dare to. I did not press him, however, and contented myself with ordering him not to touch the stitches until I arrived there at 4 P.M. to have a look at the girl myself, and that if the wound had healed, as I very much doubted, I would remove them.

Gennaro and his wife exchanged a quick look and he said, "*Va bene, signor dottore,*" and he gave me a quick, perfunctory bow and departed with his wife.

Gigetto, who had been present during my interview with the couple, informed me I had two countryside calls, and when did I desire to make them? I told him to pick me up at 1 P.M. and dismissed him.

I was curious to know more about the marquess and the

Alda family and what it was that Gennaro had appeared to want to tell me but feared to. Don Attilio smiled. Gennaro had good reason to be afraid to talk. The marquess was, for one thing, a notorious skinflint. For another, Gennaro, Alda and dozens of others owed him fairly substantial sums in the form of rent arrears, or for farm implements they had hired or supplies of one kind or another. Consequently, he had a good part of the countryside in his grip. And being a petty, cold, selfish, greedy little man, Don Attilio concluded, he was determined to squeeze every last drop of blood out of those poor, wretched people. That was what Gennaro wanted to tell me but wouldn't.

There was another thing bothering me. I didn't quite comprehend how my predecessor could have placed the operation of the infirmary almost entirely in the hands of Gennaro and his wife. Surely he must have known that their knowledge of medicine was extremely limited—and that, I added, was being quite charitable about it. How could Papini, as a doctor, have ever entrusted the care and treatment of his patients to such incompetent, untrained custodians?

Don Nicola laughed. It was a hard, brittle laugh, filled with scorn and cold fury. "That one!" he said. "He was *un pazzo,* a lunatic! Most of the time he was in a stew about something. He was always quarreling with everybody. If he was asked to go out to see a patient in the daytime, he'd complain about the sun and try to get out of it because he claimed the sun was bad for him. If it was at night, he'd empty his chamberpot on whoever it was came to summon him. Sometimes he'd throw the pot itself. He fractured one man's skull that way and then refused to treat him. Said it was the fellow's own fault. We had to get a doctor from Ancona, and that cost us plenty, plus the damages we had to pay to the injured man."

Don Attilio lit a cigar. "I wonder, though, whether he really was so crazy. He not only accepted all kinds of gifts from the patients—chickens, eggs, fruit, shoes, cheese, jewelry, anything at all—but he'd ask them for money besides, conveniently forgetting he was paid a regular salary by the town."

"And did the patients pay?" I asked.

"Some did and some didn't. A lot of the country people didn't know they were being taxed, as well as us, for medical care. In any case, whatever he managed to collect was just so much extra."

"By the way," Don Nicola said, "do you want his private key to the church?"

"What would I want that for?"

"I don't know. Your predecessor seemed to have some use for it." Don Nicola sipped his coffee. "That was another of his, shall we say, eccentricities, eh?"

"Per Bacco!" I exclaimed. "Why should a doctor need a private key to the church?"

Don Nicola shrugged. "The very day he arrived he asked me for one, so I had one specially made for him. Naturally I was curious to know what he was up to, especially since I found he was visiting the church at all sorts of queer hours. So one night I followed him. He was standing in front of the Holy Mother, absolutely motionless, arms outstretched, eyes wide-open in a kind of glassy, dead stare, his entire body as rigid as the statue itself. I watched him for perhaps ten minutes and he never moved so much as an eyelash."

"Sounds like a cataleptic trance," I said.

"And I have it on good authority——" Don Attilio began.

"Which is Filomena peeping through a keyhole!" his brother-in-law interrupted with a booming laugh.

"Precisamente! Precisely!" Don Attilio said, a trifle nettled. "Anyhow, I am told that your colleague, Dr. Papini, had a large painting of Santa Maria delle Mercede in his room before which he would kneel, stark naked, and pray for long, long, long periods—thirty, forty minutes at a stretch—and then he'd pinch himself all over, or stick needles and knives into his flesh, or put a burning match to his toes or fingers, or stick things up his ——"

"Filomena must have gotten a sore back from that much keyhole-peeping," I said.

Don Nicola smiled. "Oh, no! She'd bring a couple of pillows and sit on the floor quite comfortably."

"It was a good thing he decided to quit," said Don Attilio. "Another week and he'd have been fired!"

His wife, who had taken no part in the conversation thus far, sighed and asked me, quite seriously, whether there was anything about the practice of my profession that affected a man's mind.

"I hope not," I replied, smiling. "At least, if there is I haven't yet heard about it."

"I don't know why it is," she went on, "but it seems as if every doctor I've ever known has been—well, a bit odd. Though you certainly seem normal enough, I must admit."

"Be careful, dear lady!" I said, laughing. "You must never judge by appearances. When you really get to know me you will find that I am a veritable cesspool of bizarre vices. For example, one of my greatest delights is to devour babies alive by the light of the full moon!"

"Yes, Doctor, the moment I set eyes on you," she said with a twinkle in her dark eyes, "I said to myself, 'There is a man who likes to devour babies by moonlight.'"

That produced a loud burst of laughter, and when it subsided Don Nicola remarked that there was at least a grain or two of truth in what his sister had said about doctors. They had been rather unfortunate in their choice of physicians in Cingoli. Before Papini they had had a collection of real freaks and misfits. One had been a drug addict; another had got into trouble with a number of young girls; another with boys. And Papini's immediate predecessor had been drunk from early morning till late at night, seven days a week, and had to be discharged.

"No wonder!" Donna Letizia snapped. "My brother, out of the kindness of his heart, gave him a key to the wine cellar!"

"*Peccavi! Peccavi!*" Don Nicola murmured, rolling his eyes heavenward in mock imitation of his assistant.

"One had a key to the church, another to the cellar . . ."

Don Attilio said. "Now, I wonder, *signor dottore,* what you will be wanting—a key to the bordello?"

That provoked another good-natured laugh; then I said that might not be beyond the realm of possibility and I told them how my fortunes had been advanced in Youngstown by Madam Caroline. When I had concluded my story there was a momentary silence. Don Nicola seemed quite thoughtful.

"You know, we condemn and sneer at these ladies," he said at last, "yet in their own somewhat irregular fashion they often do many good works. Look, for instance, at that supreme symbol of sinfulness, Mary Magdalene. Her entire story occupies only a few lines in Holy Scriptures, that is all, and yet . . ." He paused, as if pondering the matter in his own mind. "Yet what a profound, what a moving effect she has had upon countless generations of men and women!"

14 : My Scalpel Becomes a Sword

ON MAY 24, 1915, Italy declared war against Austria-Hungary and broke off diplomatic relations with the Imperial German Government. I was ordered to report to Medical Headquarters at Ancona. My orders allowed me one week before going on active duty. That gave me barely enough time to clear out of Cingoli, rush back to Agnone for a few feverish days of getting my affairs in order and taking leave of my family to rush back to Ancona.

Saying good-by to Elvira and the children was the hardest job I ever had in my entire life. Farewells at such a time and under such circumstances have always been sad and painful since the first man went off to war. In this instance it was, perhaps, a little more painful and poignant than most because during every moment I spent in Agnone I was haunted by a presentiment that I could not shake off: I felt—indeed, I might almost say I *knew*—I would never see her again, never take her in my arms again, never kiss her tender lips. Yet, curiously, it was not so much that I had any feeling that I myself would not return.

My first military assignment was to the Base Hospital at Piacenza, a city about forty miles southeast of Milano and about sixty northeast of Genoa. There I was promptly appointed adjutant.

To say the least, I was bewildered. I knew absolutely nothing about the Army. As tactfully as possible I endeavored to make the commanding officer, a Colonel di Lucia, realize this. But he only frowned and said coldly, *"Tenente,* Lieutenant, in the Army we obey orders first and question them afterward." He summoned the sergeant-major and told him to instruct me in my duties. The sergeant snapped out a salute, so I did, too, though I'm afraid mine was a rather limp one. The colonel, having thus disposed of the problem, had turned his attention to some papers on his desk and didn't even look up as we marched from his office.

The sergeant-major disposed of the problem, in turn, by what I was soon to discover was a characteristic military procedure; he summoned a lesser noncommissioned officer and charged him with the task of educating me. The latter, in his turn, solved the dilemma by another typical army device: he referred me to "higher authority," which, in this case, was a ponderous 600-page tome containing all Army Regulations pertaining to the Medical Corps. That, he informed me, would initiate me into all the mysteries of my new calling.

He then conducted me to my office, a roomy, quite pleasant chamber furnished with a desk, several chairs and an empty bookcase. That done, he saluted and left me, presumably to perfect myself in the art of military medicine.

My study of the massive volume not only failed to clear up my confusion; if anything, it increased it. It was written in a special kind of language, utterly different from anything I had ever encountered in my life. Sentences seemed to stretch on and on and had a way of doubling back on themselves, so that after I had slogged through perhaps a hundred or more words I found myself back at the beginning. Not even the rules of English grammar had been more baffling and terrifying. At the end of two hours' struggle with that sinful syntax I was about ready to call it quits and ask to be transferred to the infantry. At least there all I would have to know about was shooting a gun (so I thought, naïvely).

It was at this point that my savior appeared on the scene in the person of a quiet, gentle, amiable youth with an angel's face, cool gray eyes and a soul forged of tempered steel. He was Sergeant Soricelli, and though he looked barely eighteen, he had been in the Army nearly ten years. He had been assigned to me by the sergeant, who apparently was a much more decent sort than I had given him credit for being. Sergeant Soricelli lost no time taking me in hand. The first thing he did was brush aside the book I had been wrestling with so fruitlessly. "To get anything out of that, sir," he said, "you'd have to be *un cretino,* a cretin." He gave me a big, boyish grin. "If you ever tried to follow what they tell you in there, you'd only get in trouble, because the old man makes up his own regulations whenever it suits him." He winked. "Meaning no disrespect, of course, *tenente.*"

"Of course, Sergeant," I said, smiling. (This was another thing I would learn in the course of my military experience: the universal idiosyncrasy of C.O.'s for tossing Army Regulations overboard and making up their own.) Needless to say, I was delighted to find myself relieved of further struggle with that impenetrable and frustrating book. I regarded the sergeant in very much the same way as Dante must have regarded Virgil when he took him firmly by the hand and guided him along the tortuous circles of Hell.

Soricelli possessed a combination of traits that I have found generally quite unbeatable—cynicism and charm. All questions, all difficulties, all problems he approached and handled from one basic premise: that no one expected the Army to do anything with either speed or efficiency. Therefore, so he reasoned, there was no necessity for doing anything about anything unless you absolutely had to and were forced to take some action. Although he had acquired an enormous store of information about the seemingly mysterious military machinery and had a vast amount of what would today be termed "know-how," he preferred to stall or "pass the buck" whenever he could—and that was most of the time. He also had another rule, one I particularly admired, subscribed to and applauded: never bother officers with any business of any kind if there was any conceivable way of avoiding it—and the sergeant rarely failed to find a way.

He was thoroughly familiar with the endless series of daily, weekly and monthly reports I was supposed to issue and all those I was supposed to collect from various departments. He knew when each was due and how they were to be prepared and where to get the information that had to be in each. Without a word from me, he would write them and present them to me for my signature, showing me precisely where to sign my name. Of course, I had not the faintest notion of what I was signing, and I still don't. For all I know, I might have committed myself to paying all the expenses of the Italian Medical Corps during the first World War. He was equally adept at gathering the data and statistics we were required to submit to that mysterious, invisible thing known as "higher headquarters" (a brother, I assumed, to "higher authority").

Best of all, however, he knew how to compose that strange hybrid called a "military letter" and how to prepare it in the approved, rigorously prescribed form and in that peculiarly esoteric, clipped style which seems to be common to all armies. This last talent was his most precious one so far as I was concerned, for as adjutant I had to prepare and sign a staggering number of letters, orders, reports and other documents every day. What all this might have to do with doctoring I didn't know then and still don't know. The task could have been performed just as well—probably far better—by any ordinary clerk or office manager. Why the professional abilities and experiences of a physician had to be wasted on such routine was an utter mystery to me. In time, however, I was to learn that the ways of the military mind, like the ways of God, are inscrutable to mere mortals.

About two weeks later, I was to encounter that baffling inscrutability again. Just as inexplicably as Soricelli had been given to me, so was he suddenly taken from me. He came to me one morning and showed me his orders; he was to leave the next day for the hospital in Naples.

Without him, I was thoroughly, completely lost in the jungle of Army rules and red tape. I made a brave effort to use some of his tricks; I would try to stall and "pass the buck" to another department, but invariably the problem would land right back on my desk. I tried to bluff my way through, but after about a week of it I knew I would never be able to get by. I applied for a transfer to a front-line medical unit. Since I wasn't asking for a safe, cushy rear-echelon job, it was promptly approved and Colonel di Lucia, who had no illusions about me, heartily endorsed it.

Early in August I was ordered to join a fifty-bed mule-borne field hospital that was to operate just behind the Trentino front along the far-northern frontiers. The unit was comprised of six officers besides me—three surgeons, one pharmacist, one administrative officer and one chaplain—and 120 enlisted men, of whom half were medical personnel and half mule-skinners.

Now I had little reason to complain about the Army wasting whatever small talents I possessed. The first big drive against the hated Austrians had just been unleashed and we were busy day and night, night and day, almost continuously for weeks. I had one unbroken stretch, for example, of operating for nearly eleven hours, cutting, sewing, chopping, until it began to seem more like carpentry than surgery. In addition, an outbreak of typhoid swept through our forces, and we were busy giving shots during the periods we were supposed to be off duty from the operating room.

Yet even here the inscrutable military mind manifested itself. According to directives from on high, no amputations could be performed without the approval of the senior medical officer of the particular sector. In ours it was our own C.O., Captain Bardiello. One night a near-by field hospital requested permission to do an emergency amputation on a leg that had gangrened. Obviously it was a matter of great urgency. Captain Bardiello was in the midst of operating when the request came in, so he delegated me, since I was second in command, to go in his place and make whatever decision I thought best.

I rushed to the other hospital. One look at the greenish-black discoloration relentlessly advancing up the soldier's leg told me that it must be removed as fast as possible, if the man's life was to be saved. In the name of my captain, I authorized the operation. But that was not good enough for the commander of the other hospital, even though he himself had asked to be allowed to amputate. Regulations required that the senior M.O. examine the patient personally before approving.

I hurried back. Captain Bardiello, cursing ferociously, scribbled a note on the edge of the operating table not merely authorizing me to act for him but flatly ordering the other officer to obey whatever orders I gave. But that still failed to comply with the strict letter of the regulations. I might have written the thing myself and forged the captain's signature.

Again I returned. This time Bardiello exploded. "Tell that cretin of a commander," he roared, "that if he fails to obey my verbal order, I'll have him court-martialed!"

I made a third try to the neighboring unit. But with no better success.

"He can *try* to court-martial me," the C.O. there told me, "but I cannot be punished for complying exactly with a headquarters directive. In any case, Lieutenant, I am quite willing to take that risk."

I reported this to my captain. "Headquarters directive, indeed! That idiot's following a *hind*quarters directive!"

By then it was almost 3 A.M. Bardiello had been at the table for seven solid hours. He was utterly exhausted and one of our other officers relieved him, for the wounded were still coming in without letup. Nevertheless, despite his weariness, he and I went to inspect the gangrenous leg. The whole thing by this time had taken on the grotesque and grisly aspect of the Molière play in which the doctors prefer to let their patient die "according to the rules" of medicine, rather than save him by violating all the established, orthodox procedures. When we reached the hospital we found that the problem had taken care of itself. The soldier had conveniently died.

Throughout the autumn and early winter of 1915 I remained with the field hospital. In February, 1916, I was again transferred, this time to a still more advanced position. I was appointed medical officer of an infanrty battalion stationed only some 200 yards in front of the Austrian lines at Monte Coston.

Now I got a real taste of war close up. Our battalion aid station was located less than a mile from our trenches. It was a two-room wooden hut concealed and camouflaged in a clump of trees. The larger of the two rooms was the aid station proper, containing an operating table, instrument cabinet and several makeshift beds consisting of litters set up on carpenters' horses. The other room housed my quarters. Alongside the hut was the battalion cemetery with a huge cross in the middle of it made by stripping a pine tree and nailing a log across it horizontally.

A few weeks after I joined it the regiment of which we were a part got a new colonel. He was at the front for the first time; this was his initial fighting command. Like all newcomers, he was greedy for glory. Within a week of his arrival he had persuaded division headquarters to let him mount a limited offensive for the purpose of capturing a strongly entrenched enemy position on a hill directly ahead of us. Preparations for the attack were made; a date and hour were fixed to go "over the top," and all was in readiness for the assault on Monticello, as the hill was called. It promised to be a bloody business. The Austrians occupied the position in force and their defenses were very strong; our artillery had blasted them repeatedly without dislodging them; they were dug in securely in caves, pillboxes and extremely deep, protected trenches. Naturally our men were not exactly overjoyed at the prospect of storming that strong point. For months they had been sitting there, facing their foes, without either of them suffering too serious casualties, because of a sort of unwritten, unofficial gentleman's agreement on both sides not to disturb the *status quo*. Now a fire-eating glory-grabber had to come along and upset the applecart!

But our warlike colonel reckoned without a little bug known as *Morbilli rubeola*. Two days before zero hour one of the men in the First Battalion came down with a case of the measles. As battalion M.O. I immediately quarantined the entire unit and the other M.O.'s did the same in theirs. The *colonello* was, of course, furious, and had there been any way for him to have the unpatriotic bacillus shot he would have done it. Instead, all he could do was cancel the entire offensive and wait till the bugs had raised the siege.

By that time it was too late, for the Austrians had got some ideas of their own in the interim. In mid-May they launched an offensive and forced us to retreat a considerable distance southward, inflicting rather heavy casualties. We succeeded in halting the rout, regrouping and counterattacking. By the beginning of June we were able to begin advancing and regaining a good portion of the lost ground.

About a week later, while I was operating I received a very minor wound in my leg from a shell burst about a hundred yards away, a splinter of shrapnel piercing my right calf. I slapped on a dressing and went on with my work. A short time later I was summoned to battalion HQ by the battalion commander. He informed me that I was to go on leave. I thought it was on account of my wound, but the major looked at me puzzled and said no, it had nothing to do with any wound; I was needed at home.

A sickening wave of fear swept through me. Elvira! Or the children!

Within forty-eight hours I was back in Agnone. All my very worst apprehensions proved justified. For weeks before I had been receiving letters from Elvira that were just *too* cheerful; I could not help feeling that she was covering up something, though what exactly I couldn't divine. I had been right—much too right. Elvira had begun to develop symptoms of a nervous disorder. According to Dr. Cremonese, they were not too serious. But she had worried about them; and she had worried about me. The two, together, preyed on her mind and combined with her gnawing loneliness to plunge her into a state of extreme melancholia and depression. On June 10, she had swallowed bichloride of mercury tablets. Cremonese and I labored and fought to save her. But it was a hopeless battle. On June 16, my Elvira passed away.

I took the children to Naples, following the funeral, to my sister Patrizia's. There was still more than two weeks' leave remaining, but I couldn't bear to stay among so many reminders of one whom I loved. I hurried back to the front.

This time I was assigned to a large field hospital near Feltre, a town about forty-five miles northwest of Venice that had been the principal objective of the Austrian offensive in May. There I remained till midwinter, when I was again transferred to a very small field hospital set up alongside a country road in several farmhouses. This was, fortunately, a quiet sector, and I had a splendid opportunity to recuperate from my wounds, inward and outer. In August, 1917, I was promoted to captain and assigned to still another post with an infantry battalion stationed outside Canalone di Fiammes amid the towering Dolomite Alps.

Here I more than made up for the respite I had enjoyed for a few brief months. Although I was detailed to handling medical cases only, I was kept quite busy. Here, also, I once more encountered the idiocies of the regulations-constipated military mind—if that is not a contradiction in terms.

One of my patients was a man with a severe case of hemoptysis, or lung hemorrhage. I lost no time shipping him to a base hospital in the rear with a recommendation that he be discharged from further military service. Two days later, to my astonishment, I found that not only had he been returned to the outfit but he was actually back on duty. I immediately ordered him to report to the dispensary and sent him back to the base hospital.

Within another two days he was in our midst once more. This time the battalion C.O. ordered me not to send him to the hospital a third time. When I pointed out that the man might die at any moment the colonel's eyes narrowed and he said, shrugging, "Well, *capitano,* if he's got to die, why not let him die a hero's death, on the batlefield? That way, his family would get a medal and be saved a lot of trouble and expense."

But I couldn't quite see that. After all, my job was to help keep men alive, not to hasten their deaths. So in spite of the C.O.'s orders, I sent the soldier to the hospital again. This time they didn't fire him back at us. They couldn't; he died before they had a chance.

The summer of 1917 was relatively uneventful. On October 19 we took up a new position at Padeon Nuovo. Then, on October 21, we moved on to Trecroci, a summer resort town situated at the foot of majestic Mount Cristallo not more than fifteen or twenty miles from the Austrian frontier. There in what had been a luxurious hotel we were to enjoy a three-week rest period.

Our rest was very short-lived. Two days after we arrived in Trecroci, at midnight of October 23–24, the Austrians reinforced by several German divisions launched a disastrous offensive against our Isonzo Line, our most advanced easterly position extending into Austria and what is today Yugoslavia. The breakthrough occurred at Caporetto, about one hundred miles due north of Trieste, and before the attack could be contained and stopped on November 6, the Austro-German forces had swept across the Venetian Plain and were within twenty miles of Venice. We succeeded in stabilizing our lines along the River Piave, but in that devastating two-week period we had lost almost all the territory we had won in two and a half years of bitter fighting with enormous casualties.

The communiqués called it a "strategic withdrawal," but we who took part in it knew it for what it really was—a frenzied, disorderly rout. Our battalion fell back on San Vito—Saint Vitus, a most appropriate name! From there we fell back on Vinigo; from there, on Venas; from there, on Perarolo. From there we fell back toward Montebulluna, where the High Command hoped to make a stand. From there we fell back, back, back . . .

As a battalion surgeon, I was still supposed to take care of the sick and wounded. But that had now become a hopeless, heartbreaking task. Our front-line medical installations had been overwhelmed by the enemy; our base hospitals had withdrawn beyond Venice and below Verona; all our own facilities—ambulances, equipment, medicines, instruments—had been either abandoned or lost or destroyed. As best I could, I tried to look after those that needed medical attention. But there were not too many. Only those who were so ill they could not move bothered to halt their headlong flight to receive medical treatment.

All our transportation, motorized and animal, had been swallowed up during the first two days of the retreat. For the next fourteen days we plodded south and west in a confused rabble, our progress hampered with and slowed down by the mass of fleeing civilians choking the roads. Then, on the night of November 9, as a group of my men and I reached the outskirts of the village of Faè di Longarone, a new disaster overtook us.

15 : M.D. Turned P.W.

THE GERMANS HAD TAKEN LONGARONE. We were halfway inside the town, however, before we discovered this unpleasant fact. It was too late for us to escape.

Now I found myself thrust into a new role—prisoner of war. The next three or four weeks—my sense of time became a bit vague during this phase of my life—were spent marching along snowy, wind-swept roads or riding in freezing, filthy cattlecars, having very little to eat and that rotten, being shunted from one prison camp to another. Finally, I reached the *Stalag,* or concentration camp, at Aschach in northern Austria near the German frontier. It sprawled over a large area near the Danube and consisted of eight separate sections, each filled with huge barracks constructed of tar-paper-covered wood in identical rows. It could hold 35,000 prisoners and had cost 10,000,000 *Kronen* to build. Unofficially, it was known as "the Serbian cemetery," the reason being that it had originally housed Serbian P.W.'s until epidemics of cholera, spotted fever and typhoid had carried off some 22,000 of them.

Most of the inmates would have been better off had they suffered a similar fate. Their uniforms had long since become unrecognizable dirty rags, swarming with lice and fleas, their bodies, faces and hands covered with ugly, pus-dripping sores, their eyes empty, their cheeks sunken and their grayish-green faces pinched with hunger and blank with boredom. They shuffled about, their eyes fixed to the ground—not, however, because they were thinking profound thoughts, but because they were hunting for something, anything, to eat—grass, roots, garbage, potato peels, dung, bark. And when they stumbled on some treasure they would fall to the ground and devour it greedily, watching out of the corners of their eyes for fear someone else might try to snatch the delicacy out of their mouths.

This was my first sight of long-term P.W.'s, and I was both shocked and fascinated. Everything I remembered from Dante's *Inferno* came flooding back into my mind. I thought I was in the very lowest circle of Hell.

There was a prison hospital also. At least, that was what it was called. It consisted of two wooden barracks, the green planks warped and shrunken so that the walls were a mass of gaping cracks through which the cold air poured into the interior. One barrack housed the medical, the other the surgical, ward. In the former, I saw men suffering from tuberculosis, scarlet fever, typhoid, dysentery, scabies and a dozen other highly contagious diseases lying cheek-by-jowl, one infecting the other in an endless and deadly chain reaction. Most of them had long since ceased to be men; they had become mere skeletons covered with thin, yellow parchment that might once have been human skin. They had barely the strength to move an eyelid, and speech was reduced to whispered monosyllables.

The surgical ward was equally revolting. There I saw heavily bandaged patients being carried about on the backs of orderlies like sacks of grain. They were being hauled to and from the surgery either to be operated on or have dressings changed. The reason for this dangerous mode of travel was that there were no wheeled litters or even stretchers.

As for equipment, the operating table consisted of wooden planks nailed together and mounted on a couple of carpenters' horses. There was an abundance of surgical instruments, though, but all of them were dental pliers. The only dressings and bandages were made out of paper, and for cotton they used wood shavings. Here a surgeon really had to be a carpenter! In the pharmacy, the only medicine on hand was iodine. There was, however, an impressive collection of empty bottles which, with typical Teutonic orderliness, were kept spotlessly cleaned and polished.

Like all prisons everywhere, ours was a black-marketeer's paradise. For a price, one could get anything from sex to cigarettes—the last being the more difficult and expensive. As officers, we were not supposed to do any work and therefore drew regular pay from the Austro-Hungarian government. As a captain I received 300 *Kronen* a month, and this provided me with many "luxuries" I could not have otherwise enjoyed. One of them was fresh bread—anyway, they said it was fresh and bread. It weighed about three pounds and was supposed to last for five days; that meant ten slices. Cutting it up ten ways required the skill and tools of a surveyor. It was a complete waste of time and effort, though; by the third day it was moldy and wormy and had to be thrown away.

We were also able to buy meat of decidedly dubious origin. Many of us speculated on this problem, but not too deeply. We wanted to go on eating the stuff, whatever it was. Though we did hear ugly rumors to the effect that the Austrian cat, dog and rat population had dwindled sharply since August, 1914.

My stay at Aschach was not long. Ten days or two weeks, at the outside. On December 22, I was transferred to a place called Marchtrenk. The only difference between it and Aschach was that Aschach was palatial by comparison. Marchtrenk was older, dirtier, more crowded and more verminous; in all other respects, however, it was the same. But I remained there only a little over a month. On January 30, 1918, I was again moved, this time to Mauthausen. This promised to be a decided change for the better. Mauthausen was considered the best-run of all the Austrian prison camps. Its inmates were allowed to receive packages from their families and the Red Cross. Also, and this was the thing that cheered me most, it served as a kind of clearing-house for the exchange of P.W.'s.

In appearance Mauthausen was little different from the others, save that it was much larger; it housed 70,000 men and occupied an area of some twenty square miles. It consisted of the usual eight sections and the same unvarying wooden barracks and other installations, all surrounded by barbed-wire fences, with observation towers armed with machine guns and small artillery pieces. One portion was not as securely guarded, though. This was the cemetery; apparently our captors felt that its occupants could be trusted not to escape.

I was assigned to the quarters set aside for captured medical officers. It consisted of a long, narrow barracks divided into cubicles, each holding one man. Along one side ran a narrow corridor which led to a large, clean, sunny mess hall.

For officers, life at Mauthausen was quite tolerable. The food, while not overabundant, was prepared in Italian style and was fairly edible. We had to pay three *Kronen* a day for rations, to be sure, but it was well worth it.

We were also allowed much more personal freedom, especially the medical officers, whose services were gratuitous. Hence, we could go on strolls into the near-by countryside. There was a fairly well-stocked canteen, where we could buy cigarettes, books and other items. There was a school, a laboratory, shops for shoemaking, tailoring and carpentry, a bathhouse, a theater, a cinema, an orchestra, athletic groups and two weekly newspapers. Best of all, though, was its "package service," which handled the distribution of gifts sent in from the outside.

The camp's medical facilities were equally superior. There were separate wards for surgical, medical, tubercular and all other contagious diseases. The T.B. patients were particularly blood-curdling. They were so poorly cared for that they had ceased to resemble men; they looked like some kind of grotesque larvae, wriggling and writhing in an agonizing effort to remain alive. Those who were classified as "exhausted" by the Austrians were returned to Italy as a free gift—that is, not on an exchange basis.

Leaving the hospital, I observed a small procession of P.W.'s crawling toward the cemetery. Each man carried one, or two, or sometimes even three smallish pine boxes on his shoulders. They contained the mortal remains of men who had died the previous night, packed two in the box. Nor was this seemingly difficult feat accomplished because the pallbearers were so strong. On the contrary, most of them appeared to be about ready to take the same journey themselves.

In addition to the hospital, there was an infirmary set up to handle the overflow from the larger institution. Here conditions were appallingly worse. The "beds" consisted of clumps of dirty, rotting straw splattered with old vomit and excreta. A dozen wraiths lay in this filth, mumbling incoherently, suspended in a semicomatose state, awaiting a merciful end to the pain and misery.

The dispensary was little better. There was quite a heavy sick call when I visited it, so I pitched in to help the other medical officers examine the men. One of those I looked at had a peculiar patch of color on his chest. I took a moment before I realized what it was; his whole chest was crawling with lice.

After about an hour of the dispensary I had to leave. Outside I nearly stumbled over two men intent on splitting a loaf of bread between them equally. They had rigged up a scale consisting of a wooden beam about a foot long with a nail in the center as a balance point and a wire hook at each end. Crude, but quite accurate. I watched them for several minutes as they weighed the bread with the utmost care, not even overlooking the crumbs.

From there I visited the kitchen. The first thing that struck me was a dreadful, sickly-sweet stench. I asked the cook what he was making.

"A beef stew, Captain," he said.

"*Beef* stew?" I said.

"Well . . ." He paused, hesitating, then gave me a small, crooked smile. "Anyway, it's meat. Though there's something strange about it."

"How so?"

"When I put it in the boiling water, it turned all kinds of colors—purple, green, pink, yellow."

I tried to get close to the big kettle to look at it, but I couldn't. I didn't have the stomach for it.

"What sort of meat is it?" I asked him.

"I don't really know, Captain," he replied, staring at me rather oddly, his eyes bulging. "Except somebody said it came from the front. . . ."

I had no desire to explore that subject any further.

As I continued my tour of Mauthausen I kept revising my opinion of the place, and always downward. By this point it seemed inconceivable that there could be anything worse. But there was. Within this enormous jailhouse was another jail, where prisoners who had committed any infraction of the strict camp rules were imprisoned and punished. Punishment was of two kinds: light and heavy. Light punishment consisted merely of depriving the man of all food for anywhere from twenty-four to ninety-six hours. That a goodly number died as a result of these compulsory fasts was regarded by the Austrians as simply another slightly unpleasant fact of life which they shrugged off with truly Viennese elegance and charm. Heavy punishment involved actual physical chastisement, generally in the form of whipping on the bare buttocks. Some bright mind, however, had devised a new form of torture which they called *palo,* or pole. In this, the victim was first stripped, then tied to a pole with his wrists bound tightly behind his back and fastened to the pole high above his head. His ankles, also tightly bound together, were tied to the pole about two feet above the ground. Thus, his body was bent like a bow and he was left dangling in that position for hours. If he fainted, a bucket of icy water would be thrown at him to revive him.

The enlisted P.W.'s also received a monthly stipend from the Austrians, as the Geneva Convention required. Naturally, however, it was much less than officers got, being scaled by rank as it was in our Army and in all other armies. Hence, it was far more difficult for them to obtain many items, such as cigarettes, which could be got only on the black market at exorbitant prices. In order to lay hands on extra money many of the men—most, in fact—did things they hated and were ashamed of doing. Some took jobs in Austrian munition factories, helping to make weapons that would kill their own compatriots and that would, ironically, by prolonging the enemy's power to resist, prolong the war and their own stay in an Austrian prison.

Others found it less degrading to become male prostitutes and to gratify the sexual appetites of their fellow prisoners or some of the less prudent Austrian officers. As in all places where men are confined and lack feminine companionship, the incidence of homosexuality soared and it was practiced quite openly, the camp authorities making no effort to suppress it except among their own personnel. Indeed, they rather encouraged it and capitalized on its propaganda value, employing it to illustrate their thesis regarding the "degenerate Italians." Of course, I am sure the same sort of thing was being practiced among Austrian P.W.'s in Italian prison camps and we were smugly pointing to it as an example of the "degenerate Austrians," and the same with the French, Germans, English, Russians and Americans.

One day I came across an Italian corporal, an exceptionally handsome young fellow of about twenty-five, with features that Rafaello would have delighted to paint, except for one thing. He had a deep, ugly scar bitten into his right cheek; it distorted one side of his face and interfered with the free movement of his mouth. I thought he had been wounded in battle; but such, I learned to my surprise and disgust, had not been the case. A certain Austrian major, who commanded another camp where the corporal had been imprisoned, had taken quite a fancy to the boy and had ordered him to perform a certain unnatural act. When the Italian refused, the major got furious. "Very well!" he had said. "Since you have such an aversion to it, I'll see to it you never will be able to do it." He took out his service revolver and shot him.

Another case involving sodomy occurred in Mauthausen and

had a rather grisly aftermath, which I myself observed. Two
Italian artillerymen quarreled over a nineteen-year-old infantry-
man; one of them got stabbed to death and the survivor was
seriously cut up. I had been detailed to investigate the killing
by the Italian P.W. colonel who was directly in command of the
prisoners. The floor of the barrack in which the battle had taken
place was naturally heavily splattered with blood. As I examined
the "scene of the crime" a starved-looking soldier appeared with
a tin dish and spoon. He got on his knees, began scraping the
dried blood off the floor and putting it in the dish. I asked
him what he was doing and he replied in a barely audible voice,
"Ho molto fame, signor capitano—I'm very hungry, Captain."

"But . . . but that's blood, human blood!" I said.

"Sì—I know. It will make good soup."

I was assigned, a few weeks after my arrival, to run the
officers' infirmary under the vague supervision of an Austrian
Medical Corps major. Since the officer P.W.'s had fairly comfortable living conditions—in fact, luxurious by comparison with
those of enlisted men—my biggest medical problem was psychiatric. Boredom and monotony took a terrible toll in neurasthenia,
breakdowns and other types of nervous and mental disorders.
Reduced to an empty, dull, unvarying daily pattern of existence,
the officers had sunk into a sort of spiritual quicksand which
steadily and relentlessly was sucking them down into insanity.
The only thing that helped to keep some of them from disap-
pearing into that gray void—a slender branch to which they
tried to cling with desperate strength—was the hope of repatriation.

To be repatriated (as distinguished from being exchanged),
a P.W. had to be medically classified either as "Invalid" or as
"Exhausted." The procedure involved in securing such a coveted
classification consisted of three steps: first, the would-be re-
patriate had to be examined by one of the P.W. medical officers;
second, if certified as repatriatable by the P.W. doctor, he was
next examined by an Austrian medical officer; third, if the
Austrian confirmed the Italian physician's diagnosis, a Medical

Military Commission stationed in Linz reviewed all the reports, examined the P.W. themselves, then made the final decision as to whether his case warranted returning him to his native land.

Although at least 80 per cent or more of the enlisted prisoners could have qualified for repatriation, the officers ironically found themselves disqualified, for the most part, because of the superior treatment they received at the hands of their captors by virtue of their rank. Thus, in order to achieve that blessed and greatly desired status of "Invalid" or "Exhausted," the officers had to fake it and were constantly discussing, among themselves, ways and means of "preparing for the cure." To make themselves eligible for medical repatriation they went to fantastic, incredible and dangerous lengths. Some literally starved themselves until they were "Exhausted." Others went out of their way to acquire deadly contagious diseases, and the wardmen in the T.B. and infectious-disease wards of the hospital did a thriving subterranean trade in setting up "contacts" between the officers and the worst cases on their wards. There was also a kind of underground "employment exchange" among the officers whereby they pooled information concerning the non-hospitalized prisoners who had various communicable maladies, and it became quite the thing with some of them to pay those unfortunates to permit them to practice sodomy on them, thereby, as it were, killing two birds with one stone. This was especially popular as a means of acquiring syphilis, which, in those days, was indeed a serious disease. According to camp gossip, one syphilitic enlisted P.W. accumulated some 15,000 *Kronen,* or about $3,000 at the pre-war exchange.

Horrible as that may seem, it was mild by comparison with some of the other methods employed by these desperate men. One burned out an eye with acid. Another chopped off three fingers from his hand. Another gave a hospital orderly a thousand *Kronen* for the sputum of an advanced T.B. patient and held the germ-laden saliva in his own mouth during his examination by the medical officer and then expectorated it as a sample for sputum analysis.

But "preparing for the cure" was no hit-or-miss business; it was carefully organized. There was, in fact, a regular secret "invalid school" where candidates were taught various methods of faking diseases, their symptoms, effects, causes and so on. There was a "shop" where all sorts of gadgets and devices were manufactured to assist the aspirants in simulating various traumatic afflictions. "Wounds" of one kind or another were "inflicted" here, with the aid of the scalpel, nitrate of silver and iodine. "Muscular atrophy" was effected by the application of heavy plaster casts and tight bandaging for two or three weeks. "Synovitis"—inflammation of the lubricating membranes inside joints—was produced by extremely tight bandages above and below the particular joint or by constant beating of it with small bags of sand. An "edema" or "dropsy," which normally results from an abnormal accumulation of liquid in some part of the body, was contrived by tight bindings and hot packs of physiological solution. Massive injections of cocaine or Novocain produced a reasonable facsimile of "paresis," which is manifested by a partial paralysis affecting muscular motion, but not of the sensory organs. If a candidate wished to cripple himself, this could be done without any actual faking; a bone was broken and then badly set. Injections of bismuth emulsion or persistent rubbing would produce deformed, bony calluses that could easily pass for "tuberculosis of the bones." Soap and powdered ipecacuanha, which is generally used as an emetic, when put in a man's eye would result in "granular conjunctivitis." An infusion of tobacco produced a high fever. Caustics introduced inside the ear brought symptoms that would be diagnosed as "otitis," an inflammation of the mucous membranes of the ear. By inserting non-coagulating arterial rabbit blood in the throat, a convincing replica of "hemoptysis," or lung hemorrhage, could be manufactured. Heavy doses of caffeine and sparteine produced a "cardiac condition." By smoking sulphur or sugar cigarettes or inhaling ammonia, a man could irritate his upper respiratory tract enough to cause a suspicion of "incipient pulmonary tuberculosis." Picric acid created "jaundice" and "malaria." Injections of sterile albumin into the bladder simulated "albuminuria." Salicylates, such as aspirin, resulted in "nephritis," or inflammation of the kidneys, with a consequent edema.

Nor were mental diseases overlooked. In one way they were easier to fake, in another far more difficult. Actually, to be foolproof, they required consummate acting ability plus a thorough knowledge of all the symptoms associated with the particular form of mental illness. Also, a great deal depended on the examining physician's knowledge and experience in psychiatric maladies. Nevertheless, a fairly high percentage of men were repatriated because of "anxiety neurosis," "paranoia," "religious mania," "manic-depressive insanity," "suicidal tendencies," "neurasthenia" and other nervous or mental ailments.

Still others preferred less elaborate ruses and adopted the simpler, more direct method of really making themselves sick by prolonged fasting, going without sleep, excessive masturbation or homosexual intercourse, exposing themselves to the elements, morphine addiction, massive doses of thyroxine and iodide solutions and constant use of strong purgatives. In most instances, two or more of these were combined in order to achieve more quickly a state of complete organic prostration.

Of course, the Italian medical officers always knew about the fake cases, but we carefully looked the other way, and as long as the symptoms presented a solid, medically sound picture we accepted them at face value. And whenever they failed to ring true we would advise the candidate wherein he had missed out and how to correct his "act," and naturally would not turn in our report until the man had returned and was able to pass the test. I often wondered, though, how many of our Austrian colleagues were actually taken in by those elaborate camouflages and how many did the same thing we did and out of the goodness of their hearts closed their eyes to many things.

By May, 1918, I was rapidly reaching the same state as the others. I too yearned for repatriation, and after all my efforts and pleas to obtain it on the grounds of my many months of service as a medical officer in the P.W. camps were turned down by the Austrians, I decided to "take the cure" myself. For me it was a comparatively easy matter. I selected albuminuria as the disease from which I was supposedly suffering. One of my fellow medical officer P.W.'s was my accomplice. In advance of my examination we drilled a hole through the wooden wall of the dispensary where I was to be gone over by the Austrian doctor. When it came time for me to provide him with a specimen of my urine I went behind the screen with the empty bottle. My accomplice, who was on the other side of the wall with the urine of a hospital patient who had a severe albuminuria, pushed a rubber tube through the hole, and I siphoned the albuminous specimen into my bottle. A month later, on June 10, I was on my way back to Italy.

Upon my return I was granted a month's leave, then was assigned to a military hospital in Naples, where I spent the summer doing very little work and that little quite routine. But that changed suddenly and drastically in September when the epidemic of so-called Spanish influenza hit Italy as it did the United States and many other countries at that time. Overnight, the hospital became packed with patients; without exception every one was a serious case, and the mortality was frightfully high. Like all other members of the staff, I never stopped working during that entire month and I doubt that, all told, I got more than about seventy or eighty hours sleep throughout the whole period. Then, toward the end of September, I was struck down by the disease myself. For a time it was touch-and-go whether I would pull through or not, but my naturally strong constitution won the battle for me.

While I was still recuperating from the ravages of the flu the war ended. I expected I would soon be on my way out of the Army, and as my sick leave was nearing its end I put in for a discharge. To my astonishment it was refused. Though the fighting was over, the war wasn't. At least not its aftermath. I was assigned to a variety of routine duties.

I still wanted to get out, and my desire grew in intensity with each day that passed and found me still in uniform. Nor was it merely that I, like millions of other men all over the world, was sick unto death of war, fighting, discipline and the military mind. I had another, even more potent reason: I wanted to return to America, which in a spiritual sense I had never really left and which I still regarded as my true home. So I kept battling for my discharge and finally I won it in February, 1919.

My urge to return to the United States was so powerful that I didn't even wait to get out of uniform before booking passage for myself aboard the *Duca degli Abruzzi,* sailing for New York from Genoa on April 5. Although I hated to be separated from them still longer, I decided it was wiser to let my children remain in Italy until I got settled in the States. Minnie Filomena, now eleven, was in Naples with her aunt; Joseph, now past nine, and Italo, not quite six, were in a boarding school in Siena. I went to see them before leaving, of course, and parting from them was almost as bad as going off to war again.

Spring comes early to the Mediterranean, and the morning I left Genoa was soft and balmy, the sunshine like a warm caress. It almost made me regret the step I was taking. But I knew that the future lay on the other side of the long water. I knew I should never return to Italy to live.

PART THREE

****

After you have exhausted what there is in business, politics, con-
viviality, and so on—have found that none of these finally satisfy,
or permanently wear—what remains? Nature remains.
                                                —WALT WHITMAN

16 : Paradise Regained

NOT KNOWING WHERE ELSE to go when I landed in New York, April 21, 1919, I headed back to Youngstown. My plan was to have a look around, then to decide what I wanted to do and where I wanted to do it.

Youngstown had undergone a profound transformation. It was still the same ugly, grimy, smoky, busy city it had been before the war. The mills, for two years or more in the service of Mars, had merely grown enormously, now sprawling over large areas of the landscape. The change was not of a kind, merely of a degree.

Where a marked alteration had taken place was in the commercial and residential sections. Like every American community having any pretensions to greatness, Youngstown aped New York. During my seven-year absence it had sprouted several skyscrapers. On the island of Manhattan not one of them would have been worthy of a second look, but in Youngstown they were the glory of the Chamber of Commerce and every loyal 100-per-center and civic booster. For, after all, were they not the living, visible symbols of Progress? No one, unless he was a Bolshevik, could possibly doubt or question that. And in the residential quarters that I remembered as crowded with repulsive two-story wooden structures, now I found them crowded with modern, two-story stucco or brick structures.

The most startling change, however, was in the Brier Hill section—Brianello, or Little Italy of fond memory. Only by the widest, wildest stretch of the imagination could it any longer be described as an Italian neighborhood. Almost every outward vestige of the "old country" had vanished. Most of its houses had been modernized and, in the process, subtly Americanized, though exactly how that had been accomplished I was at a loss to say. On its streets the soft, singing rhythms and cadences of the language of Dante and Verdi were rarely heard. Instead, as the older people had died out, the only tongue that echoed through its streets and in its homes was English—rather, to be more precise, American, and American of the flattest, most nasal midwestern variety. And its residents had adopted the garb and the manners of their American neighbors as well as their speech.

The Americanization process was most striking among the younger second- and third-generation women. They, like all others of their sex throughout the country, had joined the holy crusade for Emancipation, and although they had no Lincoln to remove their man-made chains, they managed quite well without one. Their mothers and grandmothers had been more than content to submit docilely to their husbands. Not so the young matrons of the early postwar era. They were neither the serfs nor the servants of their mates, but their full, equal partners who must be consulted, considered and even catered to on demand. And, much to my surprise, they got away with it; their husbands not only submitted to this domestic despotism but rather enjoyed it. The "girls" (as they liked to call and think of themselves) made generous use of powder, rouge, lipstick and mascara; they smoked like so many human Vesuviuses; they shimmied, fox-trotted and, later on, Charlestoned with the same feverish abandon as did most of their American sisters of the twenties; they bobbed their hair and copied slavishly the unflattering styles and manners (or, rather, lack of them) and bizarre slang of the "flappers"; they acquired the questionable ability to consume vast quantities of bathtub booze, much of it manufactured in our own Brianello bathtubs by former ironpuddlers and coal-heavers transmogrified into bootleggers tricked out in $25 silk shirts and Klassy Kut Kollege Klothes. They also acquired, in their unrelenting march in a dubious Progress, the art of necking and petting, which they combined with the science of confiscating their breadwinner's weekly pay envelope before he had a chance to spend a penny of it. And if occasionally some rash breadwiner ventured to rebel—or merely voiced a protest—he soon found himself being threatened with divorce, a step that would have been utterly unthinkable five years before. Yes, my compatriots had become thoroughly Americanized.

All in all, Youngstown fairly reeked with its new plump prosperity. Wherever I went and whomever I saw, it was only too apparent that those who had remained behind during the recent conflict had reaped rich rewards.

The community's professional ranks had also become not simply crowded but overcrowded with new doctors, new lawyers, new architects. The additions to my own profession were, with very few exceptions, younger men, many of them who had just been separated from the United States Army Medical Corps as captains, majors and, in at least one instance, a full "chicken" colonel. This meant, as I soon became painfully aware, that the competition was going to be quite rough and relentless. True, I had been a *capitano* myself in the Italian forces. For a while I thought that would be an asset among the Italian-born element of Youngstown. I was speedily undeceived. Not only did it not help me; if anything, it hurt me. Most of those of Italian extraction or birth were actually doing everything in their power to "live it down" and become as "100-per-cent" as possible. With them it was a case of being *plus royale que le roi,* of being more American than the Americans. They went out of their way to avoid patronizing Italian butchers, bakers and candlestick makers, and doctors were on their blacklist also. I found it more expedient, therefore, to play down my Italianness and depend more on my reputation for being an able doctor and on the loyalty of my old patients, plus my own ability to make friends among the newer crop who had come along since I had left.

By the first week of May, barely two weeks after my return from the wars, I had found an office in the same part of town I had been in before, bought furniture, instruments and other equipment, hired a nurse and hung out my shingle. I expected it would be days, perhaps weeks or even months, before I would succeed in building up a sizable volume of practice; but my friends and former patients remained loyal, and a steady stream of them came pouring in to me from the very first day I opened my office. What is more, they brought me their friends, and the friends brought their friends, and so on, and within six months I had more patients than I ever thought I could handle by myself.

During that period, one of the principal sources of new patients were young men who sought me out with worried faces because they were certain they were suffering from syphilis, chancre or gonorrhea and felt that an ex-soldier would know more about such maladies than a civilian doctor, especially one who had served in the Italian Army. They reasoned the incidence of venereal disease must be far greater in the Italian armed forces than in the American, and I would possess thus a much greater store of knowledge and experience in treating such ailments than even an American medical officer. But the majority of these worried young gentlemen were, happily, suffering from nothing worse than what I might term syphilophobia; as a result of their military service they had become rather acutely aware of venereal disease and were inclined to detect symptoms of it at the slightest provocation. Although I had every right to charge them a fee for examining them, as an ex-soldier myself I did not have the heart to charge those boys. In a way, I received a rich payment every time I saw their faces light up when I told them there wasn't anything the matter with them.

Those first months following my return to America and private practice were, on the whole, uneventful. There were the usual problems and difficulties that go along with readjusting to civilian life after a prolonged period of military service, which was further complicated in my case by the fact I had to become reacclimated not only to the United States, but to a United States considerably altered materially and spiritually from the one I had left in 1912. In some respects, I think I may have negotiated the transition more smoothly and swiftly than did many of my American friends. Perhaps this was the happy result of my possessing a rather resilient temperament. Or perhaps it was merely because of what I had gone through in the course of the past four or five years. Anyhow, for whatever reason, by the end of 1920 I felt as if I had never been away at all. My practice was solidly re-established. I was earning more money than ever before—though that was somewhat of an optical illusion, for there was that greedy goblin who turns up after every war, the High Cost of Living, to take a big bite out of every fee, aided and abetted now by a new ally, the income tax. Nevertheless, by living modesty and keeping a tight rein on my budget, I managed to save a little money.

Yet, in spite of all that, I constantly felt a gnawing dissatisfaction within me, a certain vague sense of unfulfillment. Although I was working very hard and could behold tangible results of my labors in my steadily growing practice, my enhanced professional reputation in the community and my still small, but increasing nestegg—still, deep inside, there was a feeling of discontent. Whenever I would step back from myself and take a clear, hard look at F. Michele Daniele, M.D., I had the unpleasant sensation of watching a very busy little squirrel whirling about in a cage, expending a great deal of precious energy and getting exactly nowhere. The naked, unvarnished truth was that for all my swelling practice and my increasing reputation as a doctor, I wasn't getting any nearer my goal of becoming a specialist.

Another thing that was responsible for my frustration was the aching loneliness that was my constant companion. Though it was years now since Elvira had been taken from me, there was still a huge void in my life where she had been. As never before, I now perceived the real meaning of that humorous phrase "the better half." Only by the love of a woman is a man's better self fully realized. With each day that passed the deep truth of this was brought home to me more clearly and more forcefully.

Then, too, I missed the children. Many times I was on the point of cabling to have them sent to the States; but each time I held back, knowing that it was more important that they be allowed to finish their schooling than that I should gratify my own selfish desires. But that didn't make it any easier for me to go on living alone in a cold, impersonal hotel suite, eating most of my meals (when I could find the time to eat) by myself, enjoying my occasional diversions alone.

All of these reasons were real enough and quite valid. But deep inside, though I didn't want to admit it to myself, I knew that the actual cause of my discontent was none of these. What was really disturbing me was an old, old weakness of mine— my restless spirit, my yearning for adventure, for change, for new, distant horizons. The root of my trouble was boredom; I was bored with routine, bored with a life in which there were no major problems, bored with all the people I knew, bored with my work that had long since ceased to offer me any challenge, bored with my small success, bored with medicine itself. But what I was most bored with, I think, was myself.

At this juncture I decided that I needed some kind of a tonic—a good dose of sulphur and molasses, not for my bodily self but for the good of my soul. I consulted an able physician— Dr. F. M. Daniele, by name—and he prescribed that I find some outside interest to occupy my mind and my energies—some sport or hobby or cause.

It was just about then that Margaret Sanger opened her first birth-control clinic in Brooklyn and was arrested and sentenced to prison for it. This, of course, stirred up a great deal of publicity, controversy and angry debate. Most of the medical profession were, I think, with Mrs. Sanger in her fight. Nevertheless, there was a fairly sizable segment of doctors who opposed her views; and not all were Catholics, either; quite a number were of other faiths. My own feelings and beliefs were and had been for many years very strongly in favor of curbing excessive reproduction by artificial methods. For some time before my return to Italy I had carried on a quiet campaign in favor of birth control. Now I felt the hour had come for me to step out into the open and declare myself.

Nowadays, when the entire issue is pretty much taken for granted in this country, except among Catholics, my taking up the cudgels for this cause may seem a rather tame, unexciting thing to do. Not so, however, in 1921, when it was very much a live, electric subject that could and often did produce as many sparks as Senator McCarthy did in recent history. To come out openly and campaign for it, this was not being bold and brave but just foolhardy—particularly for a physician whose practice was largely among Italian Catholics in a comparatively small community. As one of my colleagues put it, "You're not crusading, Doctor; you're just cutting your own throat!"

But as Freud has pointed out, in every one of us there is a positive and a negative personality, a creative impulse and a destructive one, a self that desires to grow, to enrich and fulfill itself and another self that desires only to destroy itself. Perhaps it was this part of my ego that was taking control of me. In any case, propelled by some deep, blind instinct, I went on with my birth-control work.

Whereas before the war I had used a certain measure of discretion and caution, now I tackled the problem boldly, openly, honestly. Before, I had contented myself with quiet, behind-the-scenes missionary work, explaining to my women patients, and some men, too, the perils and problems attendant on excessive child-bearing. At that time, I approached it wholly from the medical point of view and made no effort to introduce all the social, economic and political aspects of the question. Now, however, I was ready to take off the gloves.

First of all, I sought and obtained the aid of a great number of my non-Catholic, non-immigrant women patients, almost all of whom had come to me, directly or indirectly, through Madam Caroline (who, I discovered, had moved onto greener pastures in Chicago during the war). They organized study groups, forums, lectures. Outstanding national and international leaders in the movement were invited to visit Youngstown and discuss birth control. I spoke frequently myself, particularly at the more informal, smaller discussion and study groups, though I also delivered a number of lectures on the medical phases of the subject in both English and Italian. A panel of leading local Protestant and Jewish clergymen was formed, and they added their voices to ours. I also enlisted the support, active as well as moral, of several of my fellow practitioners.

My associates and I knew it was hopeless to attempt to convert any Catholics to our program and views, and we did not try. Though now and then other non-praying, non-paying backsliders like myself came over to our side of their own free will, uninvited.

Since the New York Court of Appeals had reversed Mrs. Sanger's conviction and ruled that it was legal for doctors to disseminate contraceptive information as a health measure, we angled our entire campaign along that line. Thus we felt we lessened our chances of coming into conflict with the law and limited the area of organized opposition to the Church.

At my suggestion and urging, we published a number of articles explaining, in clear, simple terms, the arguments in favor of birth control and stating those opposed to it and our carefully, closely reasoned replies to them. I not only wrote several of these booklets but paid for their printing and distribution out of my own pocket. I did not regret having taken up the good fight. Whatever it cost me in money, in time, in energy, was well spent, for it gave me a more than ample return in mental stimulation and deep spiritual satisfaction.

It did, however, exact other penalties, some of which were not altogether pleasant or easy to take. For one thing, my Church not only fought us on intellectual, theological and moral grounds, all of which were quite proper and within its rights; it also fought us on a purely—or perhaps I should say *im*-purely—personal basis. A subtle, subterranean word-of-mouth campaign was launched against all the leaders of the movement, which now had the avowed purpose of ultimately setting up a free birth-control clinic in Youngstown as Margaret Sanger had done in Brooklyn. Against most of those sponsoring our crusade these attacks were of limited effectiveness; but for the professional and businessmen who numbered many Catholics among their patients, clients or customers, the effects were quite serious. In a matter of weeks I began to find a noticeable drop in my practice, and when I compared notes with some of the other physicians, lawyers and tradesmen who had enlisted under our banner I found that they, too, were suffering in the same manner. Nor was there anything we could do to counteract the poison except to wait it out and hope for the best.

During the first couple of months I would ask some of my old patients, who, I had learned, had gone to another doctor, why they had left me. Had I failed to take care of them properly? Had I overcharged them? Didn't they have as much confidence in my ability? Most of them would just squirm, and look miserable, and mumble some vague, unintelligible excuse, and get away from me as quickly as they could. Once or twice a bolder spirit would tell me straight up and down he didn't like my views on the birth-control question, that he didn't approve of a Catholic doctor flying in the face of the most sacred tenets and commandments of his religion. At first I endeavored to defend what I conceived to be my own sacred right to believe what I wanted and as I wanted on a matter that was not primarily spiritual but scientific. But I soon saw that it was impossible to convince them, not of the merits of the birth-control thesis, but merely of my right as an individual citizen to believe as I would.

Then, of course, there were my Catholic colleagues to contend with; and these supposedly professional discussions were the most bitter, furious and emotional of all. In a way, I felt a little sorry for those of my fellow practitioners who were devout in their religious duty. The birth-control issue placed them in an extremely vulnerable and insecure position. As conscientious physicians, they knew, not only in their minds but in their hearts as well, that there could be and were no valid medical reasons for opposing artificial contraception and controlled reproduction. Yet their Church compelled them to oppose it and, as doctors, to combat those who favored it.

I still remember one such clash I experienced with one of my confreres, whom I shall call Dr. McGovern, since that was not his name. He was an excellent physician in every respect and an outstanding gynecologist. I had been called in to treat one of my Catholic patients who had become pregnant and whose husband, a passionate Socialist and anticlerical, had been unemployed for many months. He had scraped together a few dollars and ordered his wife to have an abortion performed; he couldn't afford to have any more *bambini;* they had four already and couldn't take care of them. The woman had refused to interfere with God's will, and she threatened to go to the monsignor and have her husband excommunicated if he forced her to go through with an illegal operation. But that had only made him laugh. What did he care if he was excommunicated? Hadn't he excommunicated himself long ago? He hadn't set foot inside a church, made confession, taken communion or partaken of any of the sacraments in twenty years or more. He, in his turn, threatened to excommunicate his wife in a far more telling manner—by walking out on her and their children altogether, if she didn't do something to stop this latest, unwanted addition to his family. Torn between immediate punishment in this life and future punishment in the next, the woman made the only choice that anyone could make. She went to some back-alley butcher who performed what the newspapers euphemistically refer to as an "illegal operation," which is, in reality, about as much an "operation" as a decapitation or a hanging. In order to comprehend its viciousness one need only be told the aborationist received a fee of $15 for his services—which was exactly $15 more than they were worth.

Septicemia promptly set in, developing into a severe case of puerperal fever. It was at this point that I was called back to treat the woman (who was one of those who had quit me as a result of the birth-control campaign). It seemed like a pretty hopeless situation. I had her taken to the hospital at once and I called in Dr. McGovern. He found her condition still further complicated by a pelvic abscess. Her womb was greatly enlarged and there were profuse, foul-smelling discharges from it. Her temperature had risen to 104.7 degrees and her pulse was extremely rapid. McGovern decided to operate and drain the abscess. It was a slim chance, and it had to be taken. Unfortunately, it proved futile; our patient died on the table.

While we were getting dressed and leaving the hospital after the operation, McGovern and I did what all professionals do in any field: we talked over the job we had just finished. Both of us were agreed on one point: that tragedies such as this one were utterly unnecessary. But we differed sharply on how they might be avoided. He believed the answer lay in ruthlessly stamping out abortionists. I insisted that would merely be attacking the symptoms, not the disease itself; it would be destroying (assuming, of course, that it really could be done) the effect, not the cause.

His chubby face became grim and his cold blue eyes narrowed. "Then what is the answer, Daniele?" he demanded.

"Stop this indiscriminate breeding," I said. "Behave like human beings, not like rabbits."

"Contraception, eh?"

"Birth control," I said.

"You're just tampering and interfering with Nature. It can't be done, Doctor!"

"Man has been doing it ever since he first landed on this earth, and successfully, too. Where would we be today if we hadn't tampered and interfered with Nature? Every dam and dike we build is an interference with Nature. Every agricultural improvement interferes with Nature. All our advances in preventive medicine and sanitation interfere with Nature by warding off disease and epidemics. Why, all these buildings around us," I went on, "they're nothing but an interference with Nature, since they protect us from the elements. If the world were to follow your line of reasoning, Dr. McGovern, we'd go back to being naked savages living in caves."

"It is also God's law," he said, as if ending all further discussion.

Which, of course, it didn't. We argued back and forth for perhaps half an hour or more, without making the slightest impression on each other's opinions.

During the course of the next eight or ten months it so happened that I had occasion to call him in on maybe half a dozen or more similar cases. They weren't all abortions, to be sure, but all of them involved women who had become critically ill through child-bearing and pregnancy. With the exception of one other, I am happy to say, we succeeded in pulling them through. Needless to say, on all those occasions I was careful to avoid any discussion of the subject of birth control with my colleague. I had too much regard for his professional skill and too much affection for him as a man to wish to place any further strain on our relationship. But one day, as we were leaving the home of a twenty-eight-year-old woman who was carrying her seventh child, he turned to me and gave me a smile that I can only call wistful.

"Dr. Daniele," he said, "I'm afraid I have a confession to make." I guessed what he was about to say, but I remained silent, waiting for him to continue. "You are quite right," he went on. "There's only one practical solution to this problem—birth control."

17 : The Fair Adventure
of Tomorrow

As THE BIRTH-CONTROL CAMPAIGN got rolling and we began to get our forces mobilized, organized and functioning smoothly and efficiently, I started to lose first my *brio,* my enthusiasm, and then my interest. My views on the subject did not alter, nor did I believe any less strongly in the cause. What simply happened—as usually happened with me—was that as we overcame more and more obstacles I became less and less concerned with the daily activities of the enterprise.

In any case, no matter what the reason or the cause, I found myself growing increasingly restive, increasingly nervous and irritable and impatient. Had I come to myself as a patient, seeking treatment, I would have advised myself to take a vacation, get a change of scene and return refreshed in body and spirit. Except that I was omitting the last part of that advice: I was telling myself to get a change of scene and *not* return.

There was also a practical reason why I began seriously considering pulling up stakes and settling in another community. My children were growing up. They were completing their education in Italy. I felt it was time that they came to America and finished their schooling here and grew up to be Americans, not Italians. For now, since 1922, I had a double motive for remain-

ing an American. I loved the United States and the freedom it
offered me, and I hated what Italy had become and what it stood
for under Fascism. I wanted no part of it, and I didn't want my
two sons and my daughter to grow up to be goose-stepping,
obedient little Fascisti.

To send for them, that was a comparatively simple thing.
What was not quite so simple was what I was to do with them
after they arrived. Obviously they would have to continue their
education. Certainly the boys would. The problem was, where?
Joseph, the eldest, would be just about ready to enter college.
Since he knew little or nothing about the United States, it would
be up to me to select a good school for him to attend.

After long and careful deliberation I decided on two steps:
first, I would enter Joseph in Adalbert College, which is part of
Western Reserve University; second, I would sell my Youngstown practice and move to Cleveland in order to be near Joseph
while he was going to school.

It was not difficult to dispose of my practice and to obtain
an excellent price for it. In the twenties, of course, it wasn't
difficult to sell anything at any price. Mine, however, was a
pretty good practice—it had been netting me close to $20,000
a year, which was pretty good in a small town like Youngstown.

I was quite lucky in Cleveland, too. Even though it was
fairly close to Youngstown and over the years I had got to know
quite a number of Clevelanders, I still expected I would have a
rough time getting established there. But I was extremely fortunate. Some time before, I had become acquainted with Vittorio
Trutta, secretary of the Italian consulate in that city. A suave,
charming, cultured gentleman, he had been largely instrumental
in getting me to make the move. He had kept telling me there
was a need for another good Italian doctor to help look after
Cleveland's large Italian population. At least 50 per cent of the
success I enjoyed there I owe to his devoted and unremitting
efforts. Within six months after I had set up shop there, it was
as if I had been practicing in Cleveland all my professional life.

As soon as I saw that things were going to move well I

began to make arrangements to bring my children to the United States. There was no problem about getting Joseph here, for he had been born in this country and was therefore an American citizen. But my youngest, Italo, had been born in Italy, and I ran into some snags on both sides of the water. On this side, there were complications resulting from technicalities in the immigration regulations, technicalities that I never was able to unscramble or comprehend. On the other side, it was a matter of his serving his term of prescribed military service. Naturally, all this involved yards and yards of red tape. But there is always one sure, universal solvent for red tape, a lubricant that will set the wheels of every bureaucratic machine spinning smoothly and swiftly. With the assistance and counsel of my friend, Trutta, plus that of several influential American friends, I hastened to apply this magic formula. Within a relatively short time it began to produce results.

As for my daughter, Minnie Filomena, there were other problems, not of a legal or political nature but of a romantic kind. As she had also been born in Youngstown there was no difficulty about her re-entering the United States. But she had fallen in love—with a young doctor in Agnone, of all things!—and had got herself engaged. She wrote me and asked if I would mind her remaining in Italy until she was married, after which she and her husband would come to America. Although I very much wanted to have her with me too, I told her she had my blessings.

It has been well said that just about every truth known to man may be found either in Shakespeare's works or in the Bible. Thus I can think of no better way to sum up the period of my life that I was now about to enter upon than to quote those lines the king speaks in *Hamlet* after he has witnessed Ophelia's madness:

> When sorrows come, they come not single spies,
> But in battalions.

And so they did.

First of all, there was the sudden death of my dear friend, Vittorio Trutta. Less than a month before, I had given him a regular semi-annual checkup and had found not a thing organically wrong. Then, without a moment's warning, a severe heart attack, and it was all over.

I mourned his loss doubly. He was a wonderful person, a man of wide culture and discriminating tastes, one who truly exemplified and personified that very much overworked adjective *simpatico*. He had been one of the finest friends I had ever had. Then, too, his passing was a heavy blow to me for a purely practical standpoint. He had been of enormous help in getting me launched in Cleveland and in seeing to it that there was always plenty of deep water under my boat. Vittorio had never stopped boosting me and recommending patients to me. With him gone there would be a big difference.

Not that I expected to or would lose the patients he had been responsible for sending my way; but the steady, constant flow of new ones would stop. And this came at a crucial time. I had reached the period in life—I was getting uncomfortably close to the fifty-year stripe—when it was anything but easy to go out and hustle and enlarge my practice. Then there was the problem of my future son-in-law. Of course, if my daughter and he came to America, he could assist me if he wanted to. But that raised other problems, in turn. My practice as it stood could take care of two men, provided they both did some belt-tightening and penny-pinching for a while. And my promised son-in-law would have a wife to support and within a fairly short time one or more *bambini,* if I knew anything about Italians. Besides which, there was still another question that worried me: what kind of doctor was he?

My anxiety over my intended son-in-law's fitness to practice medicine in this country proved quite needless. In the September following Trutta's death I was struck down by yet another and far worse blow. One sunny morning, just as I was about to make my round of calls, a cablegram arrived. I ripped it open. The words I saw printed on that piece of paper were utterly fantastic. My daughter was dead! She had contracted typhoid. Within a matter of days she was gone. At the age of nineteen!

Let us pass over those next weeks and months quietly, quickly. How, after all, can one describe all the great, powerful emotions of life, save in tired platitudes? For weeks and weeks I drifted about like a rudderless, dismasted ship, helpless to avert total wreck on the shoals of despair. I knew that for such mortal illnesses as this there was but one sovereign specific: work, work, more work, and still more work! I knew that if I was to save myself and everything I had built over many long, hard years I must throw myself into my practice as I had never done before. I must wear myself out physically, so that each night I wouldn't *go* to bed—I'd *drop* into bed. Only by unremitting work would I be able to keep from thinking.

All this I knew, only too well. But I was powerless to fill my own prescription. I was too weak. I was too soft. I was too filled with self-pity. Instead, I brooded. I kept tormenting myself with thoughts of all those loved ones whom I had lost—first my beloved mother, then Elvira, then Vittorio Trutta, now Minnie Filomena. Those battalions of sorrow had swept over me, crushed me utterly.

I began to get careless about observing my regular appointed office hours. Patients came to see me and found that I was not there, and after a while they just stopped coming. Then I began to refuse outside calls, forcing patients to summon other doctors, and invariably they remained with the new doctor and did not return to me. For that who could blame them? Presently, as the weeks rushed by, my practice dropped sharply. Within a space of less than two months it had diminished by more than 50 per cent, and it was shrinking every day.

Meanwhile my two sons had arrived from Italy. Joseph had entered Adalbert and was making excellent progress; and Italo was going to high school and rapidly learning English. During this period of earthly purgatory they were my sole comfort and my sole incentive for going on with the bitter, uneven battle. Without them by my side I am sure I would have been lost.

As a consequence of this piling up of disasters and frustrations, I became increasingly irritated and confused. Everything and everyone got on my nerves. Without warning, without the least provocation, I would flare up and get angry and abusive with whoever happened to be present, even if it was a patient. And the very fact that I knew I had lost all control over my emotions and temper only made me all the more furious with myself, and that, in turn, only caused me to become more violent and jumpy.

My practice had gone to hell, of course, and living in Cleveland was growing more and more unbearable every day. There were too many memories, too many reminders. . . . At all costs I had to escape from what had turned into a veritable torture chamber.

18 : From Rubber Tires
to Rubber Checks

IN MY DESPERATION, I turned to what seemed like the nearest refuge—Akron. It was only about thirty miles south of Cleveland and forty-five miles due west of Youngstown. I felt I would be far enough away so that I could put the past behind me and still be close enough to old friends, should I need help, and to my boys. I should have known better; I should have known that painful memories do not dwell in houses or among green fields: they dwell only within ourselves. There are only two things I can remember about Akron—the nauseating odor of burning rubber and the dense, gray pall of smoke that never lifted from the city and through which the sun never was able to pierce.

Somewhat to my surprise, I was able to start building up a fairly respectable practice—that is, insofar as the number of patients was concerned. Income was another matter. Most of those who sought my services were of the poorest immigrant class, not only Italians but Poles, Hungarians, Czechs and Russians—the "coolie" labor of the big rubber factories. With the Italians I naturally had no difficulty. But treating those of other nationalities presented problems. I couldn't speak Polish, Russian, Hungarian or any of the other barbarous Central European languages. I found myself having to depend on sign language or on my imagination and intuition to discover what my patients' specific symptoms might be. After a while, I began to feel more like a veterinary treating dumb animals than a physician ministering to human beings.

That I became depressed and discouraged in Akron was no wonder and should occasion no surprise. The only wonder, as I look back on that episode, is how I managed to stand it as long as I did. But finally I had enough and was ready to move again.

This time, however, there was no problem as to where I should go; I had made up my mind. I wanted to go to California. The bleak, icy, damp midwestern winters were getting me down. I was over fifty and I was tired, worn out, disillusioned. On top of the personal losses I had recently experienced came the stock-market crash and then the depression. Luckily I was one of the very few people in the United States who had not played the Wall Street roulette wheel.

Another source of considerable worry to me was the houses I still owned in Youngstown. I had never been able to unload them. Once, during the boom years after the war, I had had a chance to get rid of them at a loss of maybe a couple of thousand dollars. But everywhere values were skyrocketing and all my friends in the real-estate business advised and urged me to hold on for the "long pull." Well, the "long pull" came, all right; only it was a downward pull. Though, Lord knows, it certainly was a long one! By 1930, the property wasn't earning enough to pay the taxes, and ultimately I just couldn't afford to hold it any longer and had to let it be taken over for taxes.

Another thing that decided my move to the West was Joseph. The Cleveland climate proved even harder on him than on me. His schooling was constantly being interrupted by prolonged sieges of grippe, sinusitis, colds and other respiratory ailments.

So, despite all the warnings and pleadings of my friends, I scraped together what little remained of my lifetime savings, packed my few worldly possessions, gathered my two sons and started West.

To say that I found it something less than the "earthly paradise" described in magazine advertisements and Chamber of Commerce literature would be a gross understatement. If I were forced to sum up its total effect in a single word, I would unhesitatingly say "dull." To be sure, the climate was mild and there was sunshine (those were the days before heavy industry migrated there and created the "smog" problem), all as advertised. But they somehow lacked any stimulating, invigorating qualities. The California brand of sun and atmosphere was quite different from the Italian. Italy's sunny warmth seemed to have the effect of a heady, sparkling, dry wine, as its long history of culture and productivity bears ample witness. California's, on the other hand, seemed only to slow down, to slacken and stultify, the tempo of life.

This was best evidenced by the people who had settled in and around Los Angeles. To me, as I strolled about its rather shabby, uninteresting streets, it seemed like one enormous open-air lunatic asylum. But what struck me more than anything else about Los Angeles in the 1930's was its artificiality, its air of insubstantiality. Everything had a feeling of impermanence about it, as if it were made only out of plaster, lath and papier-maché and were merely a false front for a movie set. And in nothing was this more true than the majority of its citizens. During that unfortunate period in its history it became a vast dumping ground for deadbeats and four-flushers.

Of course, I soon found my feelings toward Los Angeles promptly reciprocated and with interest. The bulk of the Italian colony there was of northern Italian extraction, and their attitude toward anyone from the southern regions of Italy was something less than enthusiastic. It is a fact not generally known outside Italy, but there has traditionally existed a marked hostility between the northern and southern sections of the nation, just as in the United States or, for that matter, between northern California and southern California. North Italy has always been the center of heavy industry, while the South has been predominantly agricultural. The North is more progressive, more modernized, and has a generally higher living standard and a higher degree of literacy. The South has always been traditionalist, monarchist and strongly Catholic.

I opened a small office in a profesional building on South Broadway and waited for my patients to come to me. During my first month I treated exactly five people, three of whom were passers-by who felt they needed immediate medical attention and went to the first doctor they found. Never before had I run into a situation like this. Everywhere else I had hung out my shingle —Youngstown, Akron, Cleveland—the local *paesani* loyally flocked to my aid at once. At the end of my first three months in "paradise" I took stock of my position. I found that my total gross earnings during that period amounted to just a trifle more than my average weekly take in Ohio.

I knew when I was licked. I decided, first, to give up my office. Accordingly, I ran several advertisements in the County Medical Association journal. The replies I received were utterly fantastic, but quite in keeping with the spirit of the place and the times. I got any number of offers to help promote various magical elixirs, mechanical devices, ointments, mystic potions. A pair of ex-barbers wanted me to use a salve they had concocted that would cure any and all types of rheumatism and related ailments. I also was invited to "front" for a dozen different kinds of shady "institutes" and private hospitals ostensibly devoted to treating alcoholics, drug addicts, homosexuals and other poor unfortunates who could be blackmailed through and because of their weaknesses. Not a single legitimate hospital or sanatorium answered my ads.

Meanwhile, in spite of the undeniably low living costs, my savings were steadily melting away. Even in southern California during the Depression years it cost *something* to feed, clothe, house, educate and take care of two boys as well as myself. No matter how rigorously I pared down my needs and how strictly

I economized, I was eating up my shrinking reserves every day.

In desperation and panic, I began casting about in any and all directions for some means of earning a living, and some of the directions were pretty weird. I'm afraid poor old Hippocrates would have blushed, if he could have known some of the so-called "opportunities" I seriously considered.

One day a salesman whom I shall call Joe Trotter, just to give him a name, met me on South Main Street. Joe worked for one of the large pharmaceutical concerns, so he got around a bit among the medical profession. We had become rather friendly and he knew my plight, was eager to help, if he could. He gave me a tip. There was a certain Dr. Martin (that wasn't *his* name, either) on whom Joe called and who was one of his best customers. He didn't know what kind of practice Dr. Martin had, whether he was a G.P. or a specialist, or, if he specialized, what his specialty might be. But one thing he did know was that Dr. Martin did "one hell of a land-office business." His waiting room was crowded, according to Joe, day and night.

Without a moment's delay I hurried over to Dr. Martin's office, which occupied most of an entire floor in one of the most expensive downtown office buildings. The waiting room was filled with patients, and a veritable flying squad of attractive young receptionists in trim, crisp white uniforms were busily ushering them into what I presumed must be the consulting rooms, for it was obvious he must have a fairly sizable staff of assistants to handle such a practice. That definitely cheered me up and gave me a solid feeling of hope for the first time in many, many weeks.

There were, however, one or two things that puzzled me a bit. For one, all the waiting patients appeared unusually happy and bright, and anything but sick. No matter how ill a person may happen to be and how much he may desire to have his suffering eased, he never looks pleased while he is sweating out an appointment with a doctor or a dentist.

Then there was another thing that seemed, I thought, a trifle odd. One of those lovely young creatures in white came over to

me, motioned me to a comfortable chair and asked me to wait a
few minutes; it wouldn't be very long before someone would take
care of me. But she did not ask my name, my address, the nature
of my complaint or anything about my medical history. And
when I said I wanted to see Dr. Martin, she gave me a great big,
gleaming smile and said yes, it wouldn't be too long a wait.

Well, I waited. Ten, fifteen minutes passed. I studied the
others sitting about the reception room. It struck me that all of
Dr. Martin's patients were men. Could it be that he specialized
in venereal diseases? I wondered. Then something else struck
me. After each was finally admitted to the inner temple he never
again reappeared; apparently there was a rear exit to the suite of
offices. For some reason, Dr. Martin did not want waiting patients to see those departing.

At last I was ushered through the double doors. I found myself in a long, dimly lit corridor on each side of which were
about a dozen doors. My mind leaped back over the years to a
summer's night in Youngstown and Madam Caroline's.

The luscious redhead who was my guide led me through one
of the doors. The narrow cubicle on the other side of it was
bare of anything save a leather-padded examination table, a chair,
a table and a hatrack.

With a brisk, professional air the girl pulled out a fountain
pen and prepared to fill in a rather large, impressive-looking card.
What was my name and address? By this time I sensed there
was something fishy going on, so I gave her a fictitious name and
address. "What's bothering you, big boy?" she then asked, smiling suggestively.

"Rheumatism," I said.

She nodded with the air of an eminent Viennese specialist
concurring with a country doctor's diagnosis. "Good! Massage is
just the thing for you," she said. "Get your clothes off, big boy,
and I'll send one of the girls in to give you a treatment." She
winked. "The fee will be two dollars—*payable in advance.*
Understand?"

"Yes, I understand," I said.

She gave me another toothy smile and disappeared.

It was now quite clear to me why Dr. Martin did "one hell of a land-office business" and what the nature of that business really was. As soon as the redhead vanished I tiptoed out of the room and hurried down the hall and got out of there as fast as I could. I was desperate—but not *that* desperate.

As the weeks wore on and the prospects of establishing myself in Los Angeles grew dimmer and dimmer, I began to ponder other solutions. For a while I even considered abandoning my profession altogether; indeed, I must be absolutely frank and confess that I did try to find work as a cashier, a clerk and a number of other assorted occupations. But nobody would have me in any of those jobs. I lacked "experience" and "training." In 1931 and 1932 prospective employers (a seemingly vanishing breed of men) could afford to be choosy. Large department stores, for example, hiring temporary Christmas sales help were not content to have graduates of Harvard, Yale, Princeton, California, Stanford and Chicago working for $14 and $16 a week, but insisted that they be graduates of engineering schools in order to demonstrate toys.

Finally I sought out an old friend and colleague, Dr. Alessandro Jardini, and asked his advice.

"You're wasting your time here in L.A.," he told me. "This isn't the place for you."

"You mean you think I should go back East?"

He shook his head. "Not at all! What I mean is that I feel you'd be better advised to set up shop in one of the smaller towns in California. Everybody gravitates to L.A., Pasadena, San Diego and the other larger communities. Most people steer clear of the smaller places. They seem to have the notion there's more opportunity in the big centers. That just isn't true."

"What makes you so sure I'll be able to get started in a little hick town?" I demanded. "Isn't there just as much likelihood of my getting stymied there as here?"

"Of course, of course," he replied. "But I'm not telling you to bury yourself in a hick town. Just because a place happens to be small doesn't necessarily mean it's dead. There are any number of towns that aren't big but that are lively hustlers and are building and growing, in spite of this Depression."

"What ones, for example?"

"Gosh! I guess I could name a dozen or more—Whittier, for instance, or Bell, or Torrance. And most of them are short-handed when it comes to doctors. And another thing—smaller communities are much more inclined to give a newcomer, especially a medic, a neighborly helping hand."

"Got any particular place in mind?" I asked.

"Well . . ." He shrugged. "There's a fairly large Italian colony around Bell. That's only seven miles south of here. Why don't you take a ride down there and have a look at it? It might pay you."

The next day I drove down to Bell. It was love at first sight. True, it was a fairly small place; its population wasn't more than 10,000, if that much. I had never practiced in any community that small in the United States. But I would be living and working among *paesani* again, for almost all the Italians there were farmers and largely from southern and central Italy, and always I had got along well with them.

It meant making another move and admitting and accepting still another stinging, humiliating defeat. But what was the good of pretending, of trying to kid myself along? It seemed far wiser to be honest with myself, take my licking like a man and attempt to retrieve something out of the wreckage.

But before I decided on any course of action, I would talk it over with my sons. They were old enough to take part in such important decisions, for one thing; and since whatever course was determined on would affect them and their future, they had every right to have a voice in it. The following night I summoned them to a council of war.

19 : Travels on a Treadmill

THE RESULT OF THE FAMILY CONCLAVE was an unanimous and very enthusiastic aye. And I lost no time carrying out this popular mandate. The next day I went back to Bell and by noon had rented a tiny suite in the Alcazar Building which would serve as combination office and living quarters. We would be quite cramped, to be sure, but at least I would be a doctor again, and that was worth all the discomfort and sacrifice in the world.

But I soon discovered that I wasn't going to ring any bell in Bell. During the first four or five weeks that microscopically small office was, if anything, far too large; I don't think I saw more than three patients in that entire time and two of them, ironically enough, were from Los Angeles. When that strange perversity that seems to be an Italian characteristic, they had never called me when I was located almost within spitting distance of their homes, but waited till I had moved nearly ten miles away. But the way things were going for me—or rather, *not* going—I raised no objections on that score. Neither I nor any other physician during those dark Depression days was doing any gift-horse looking-in-the-mouth. We asked only two things of a patient: one, that he really be sick (and some of my colleagues weren't too insistent on that qualification); two, that he have the ability to pay his bill.

It seemed to me, however, after I started building up something that resembled a practice, that while my patients more than filled the first specification, they signally failed to fill the second. The worst part about it was that they weren't deadbeats or bad-check artists, either; they just didn't have any money— a shortcoming that was all-too-common in the 1930's. Most of them were farmers, of course, so instead of paying me with cash they paid me in eggs, fruit, chickens, vegetables, milk and whatever else they produced. That would have been all right, too, if only the landlord, the pharmaceutical houses, the bank and everyone to whom I owed money would have been willing to receive payment in kind or to accept medical services. But at least we all ate well, and that was more than a great many people could say in that unhappy time.

I compared notes with two other practitioners in Bell, both of whom had been practicing there for quite some time. They were not doing much better than I was; that was some comfort and helped bolster my sagging morale a bit, though it didn't make it any easier for me to pay my bills.

About a year later Italo finished high school and Joseph was ready to go off to medical school; and since Italo would have to live in Los Angeles in order to attend U.C.L.A., that meant I would be alone again. I was reluctant to make still another move; God knows I had made too many of them in the past eight or ten years. Therefore I determined to stick it out by myself in Bell. After all, though I wasn't setting the Pacific Ocean on fire, I was getting by, and in 1932 that was about as much as anyone dared ask.

But I reckoned without that private devil of mine, restlessness. Within a couple of months I felt lost and utterly miserable. Bell had become intolerably empty; every moment I had spent there I had been starved for stimulating intellectual provender and activity. Going to the movies twice a week, talking shop with my two colleagues or exchanging neighborly gossip with my fellow townspeople just failed to fill the bill. And most of all, I missed my boys. It was especially frustrating to know that one of them was only a few miles away and yet I could see him only at infrequent intervals.

At last, in sheer desperation, I decided to chuck everything— not that there was very much to chuck—and go back to Los Angeles. In March, 1933, only a few days after the New Deal was born, I set up a combined office-apartment in Hollywood. Now I was only a short distance from Italo.

But the pattern of the recent past repeated itself once more— as I suppose I should have known from the start. Patients were so scarce that I began to think disease and death had been banished. And the few who did consult me either airily informed me they'd pay me "as soon as things picked up a bit" or presented me with more of those sun-kissed rubber checks.

And now a fresh battalion of sorrows was preparing to charge upon me. One night in mid-September, 1934, I got a phone call. A strange voice told me she was calling from St. Vincent's Hospital. Italo, she said, had been stricken with acute appendicitis and my colleague and good friend, Dr. Thomas Chalmers Myers, was going to perform an emergency operation in less than an hour. He had instructed her to notify me.

I rushed to the hospital. My first thought had been, of course, to watch the operation, and Dr. Myers had invited me to be present. But I just couldn't do it; though I had performed and observed hundreds of operations without being in the least affected, the idea of seeing my own flesh and blood cut into was more than I could bear. I sweated it out in the waiting room. The appendix was a very "hot" one, Myers had warned me, and it was not going to be an easy case. Italo was on the table for an hour and forty minutes, though to me, going through the long agony of waiting outside the operating room, it seemed more like ten hours or even ten days. Any number of times I was almost on the point of tearing into the O.R., snatching the instruments out of the surgeon's hands and finishing the job myself. I even got as far as the swinging doors, but each time I halted, not daring to move an inch further. What on earth was Myers doing, anyway? He was a good surgeon—or was he?

Why was he taking so damned long? It is a simple, quick business, an appendectomy. What kind of butchery was he inflicting on my boy? Then I heard Italo moan. Or was it only my imagination?

I went back to the waiting room and sat down and prayed—for the first time in many, many, many years. Presently the O.R. doors swung open and they wheeled Italo out. I accompanied him to his room and waited for him to come out of the anesthetic . . . wondering if he would. Finally he opened his eyes. He saw me and smiled wanly. I felt his pulse and counted his respiration again while the nurse took his temperature. The moment she had removed the thermometer and wiped it off I insisted on seeing it. Ordinarily she would have ordered me out of the room, and she would have been quite justified, but under the circumstances she merely handed me the thin sliver of glass without a word. His temperature was high, above 103 degrees, but that was not alarmingly high, considering he was postoperative and there had been serious complications.

For four days and four nights I never left that hospital. At the end of that time, Italo was definitely out of danger and making a good recovery. When Dr. Myers made his evening rounds he told me I ought to go home and get a night's sleep for a change. I said no, I felt I ought to spend one more night at least by Italo's bedside, just to make certain he was completely out of the woods.

"What are you trying to do, Mike," Dr. Myers said with a little laugh, "grab my patient away from me?" He insisted that I go home and rest. Italo was doing fine; there wasn't a thing to worry about.

I went home. By now I was utterly exhausted, not only physically, but mentally and emotionally. I fell on the bed with all my clothes on and dropped into a profound stupor.

Suddenly a bell was jangling away somewhere off in the distance. . . . I groped through a cottony fog to get back to consciousness. The bell kept jangling. Then abruptly I became awake and aware; the phone—it was the phone ringing.

It was still dark. I switched on the light alongside my bed. The alarm clock said it was 4:20 A.M. The impersonal, antiseptic female voice on the other end of the wire told me that Italo had taken a sudden turn for the worse.

I didn't wait for her to finish. I slammed down the receiver. I rushed down into the deserted, deathly still street. After 10 P.M. Los Angeles was a city of the dead. There were no cabs on the streets. I had to walk—or run—all the way to St. Vincent's.

Fortunately Dr. Myers was already by Italo's side when I got there. He got him under an oxygen tent without delay. For the next twenty-four hours Italo's life was reduced to a mere question mark. Then came the crisis. Thanks to God's mercy and Italo's strong constitution and his will to live, he surmounted it.

It was weeks later when he finally was well enough to leave the hospital, and still more weeks of slow, steady convalescence before he could return to school. Meantime I was now faced not by a mountain but a whole Alpine range of bills and debts—all of those resulting from Italo's illness on top of all those that had been relentlessly piling up during the months and years before. It was quite true that Dr. Myers sent me no bill; neither did his assistant nor the anesthetist. But there was still the hospital to be reckoned with, and the special private nursing, and the medication, and the X-ray, laboratory and other miscellaneous charges. And, alas! those were the days before hospitalization plans; it all had to come out of my hide, of which there was precious little left.

Again feeling that the only solution to my dilemma was to find something that would provide me with a regular, guaranteed income, no matter how small, I hunted for some sort of medical staff position. I was delightfully surprised, after less than two weeks' search, to be offered the directorship of an electro-therapeutic institute. The salary that went with it did not measure up to the resplendent title, but it was enough to meet my needs and leave a little over to pay off my obligations. I accepted the post with alacrity and enthusiasm, not alone because it would pay me a living wage but also because it offered me an opportunity to explore what I believed was an important new field of medical knowledge.

But once again I was doomed to disillusionment. The "institute," I soon learned, was just another one of those typical Los Angeles quackeries. They had a battery of Rube Goldberg machines that looked as if they came straight out of the laboratory of the mad scientist in one of those horror movies. They were impressive and quite fearsome to behold; they made strange noises; they threw out sparks and showed green and purple snakelike waves dancing on screens in darkened rooms. With this formidable array of equipment, the operators of this establishment advertised "cures" for everything from the common cold to cancer, from indigestion to tuberculosis, and their patients not only believed them and paid anywhere from $10 up for a single treatment, but were grateful and felt privileged to be permitted to receive treatments.

It took me not more than two days to see what it was all about and what my role was to be. I was hired only to "front" the enterprise, to give it a dignified, respectable façade of ethical medicine. Not only was I not expected to have anything to do with the actual operation of the place; I was specifically ordered to keep out of it. The salary I was getting was simply for the use of my name and title in their expensively engraved letterhead and to serve as whipping boy and scapegoat should they run afoul of the law or the American Medical Association. Not if but when that occurred, I would discover the entire responsibility dumped on my shoulders.

Of this I wanted no part. I promptly tendered my resignation as of now. I had the somewhat grim satisfaction of writing my letter of resignation (the one and only piece of correspondence I wrote during my very abbreviated stay) on one of those elegantly printed letterheads, in the upper lefthand corner of which was engraved in chaste, shiny black script *F. Michele Daniele, M.D., Medical Director.*

Quitting that job was fine for medical ethics and my professional principles, but it didn't do my pocketbook or my morale

much good. I was right back to where I'd started, pounding
the pavements, hunting for a means of scraping out a livelihood
for myself and my family. Nor did it do me any particular good
to know that I was in the same boat with millions of other
Americans.

There is neither point nor purpose in reciting all the fruit-
les efforts I made, all the barren scents I pursued, all the vain
hopes and futile ideas I cherished during this long, bitter period.
The pattern of the next four or five or six years of my life was
monotonously the same and monotonously unsuccessful and
empty. There was many a time in the course of those years when
I seriously contemplated putting the final period to what had de-
generated into a discouraging, depressing story. It would have
been easy for me to do, as a doctor. And quite painless, too.
Sometimes I wonder what kept me from doing it. The "will to
live," most people would say; but I've always felt that it is not
so much the desire to survive that keeps most of alive as it
is a sort of curiosity. We want to know what's waiting for us
just around the corner. Maybe—who knows?—it may be better
or, at least, more interesting and exciting than what we have
now. In my own case, I feel sure that was the thing that kept
me going during all those downhill, degrading years. What
would I find around the bend of the road?

What I found finally was a cataclysm of incredible magni-
tude and terror.

20 : *Mars Summons Apollo Again*

I WAS HAVING my customary late Sunday breakfast and was lingering over my third cup of *caffè nero* and glancing over the paper. It was a clear, sparkling December day. The radio was on, tuned into the regular weekly broadcast of the New York Philharmonic Symphony. I was in that pleasant state of suspension that follows a good breakfast and a relaxed frame of mind. I was reading the newspaper and only half-listening to the beautiful music that came pouring out of my radio. Suddenly, however, the sound stopped dead. For a second I thought something had happened to the set; maybe a tube had blown out. But a moment later it was playing again. Only this time, in place of the rich sounds of the orchestra, there was a voice, a man's voice. It was curiously quiet, curiously deliberate and grave. I say "curiously" because it generally took so little to make radio announcers become hysterical and dramatic—the opening of a new supermarket, the latest movie marriage or divorce. That is what made this announcer seem somehow peculiar. His voice was calm, unhurried, undramatic, yet there was also a note of solemnity and awfulness in it. He announced that Pearl Harbor had been bombed by the Japanese.

The next day we were at war, not only with Japan but with Germany and Italy as well. For us who were Americans of Italian birth or ancestry it was indeed a difficult, delicate pre-

dicament we now found ourselves in. Ever since Mussolini's
infamous "stab in the back" the year before, most of us had
been on the defensive. Even though we had loathed, opposed and
despised the bogus Caesar and everything he stood for, and even
though most of our American friends and neighbors were well
aware of our anti-Mussolini, anti-Fascist and anti-Italian sentiments, yet we still felt self-conscious and guilty about our Italian
blood and our Italian heritage. Just as we also knew that the
Italian people, out of desperation and out of indifference and
indolence, had allowed themselves to be corrupted by a gang of
killers, grafters, degenerates and lunatics. Whereas the *Führer's*
and the tyranny were the natural expression of the Germanic
mores and culture, for us it was essentially a foreign, ill-fitting,
abnormal pattern. Yet in the eyes of the world—in the eyes of
our own neighbors—we too had been made to appear, by the
damning but not altogether unjustifiable process of "guilt by
association," like monsters.

I lost no time volunteering my services to the war effort. I
went to the Los Angeles Police Department and was immediately appointed a medical member of the Auxiliary Police and
instructed to be prepared for instant duty in the case of an air
raid or any other emergency. Now all sorts of jobs began to
spring up, like mushrooms following a heavy rain. This gave
me a rather bitter satisfaction. Only a few months before I had
been regularly turned down for medical positions on the ground
that I was sixty-two years old and "younger men" were required. As the armed forces began draining off medical talent,
age no longer was such an insuperable handicap. On the contrary, almost overnight, as if by magic, age acquired enormous
value.

During the months after Pearl Harbor I enjoyed the ineffable
satisfaction of refusing at least half a dozen good job offers. And
not simply refusing them, but having people plead with me to
accept positions that paid anywhere from $10,000 to $25,000 a
year. It was, you might say, a case of a Daniele come to judgment, but with reverse English. But I had another and far

more important reason for not wanting to accept a job: I had been seized with the notion—yes, call it crazy, if you like—of going into the United States Army as a medical officer.

Italo, who had been in the Reserves, went on extended active duty as a first lieutenant in the Army Medical Corps in August, 1942, and was ordered to Fort Ord in northern California. Joseph, who also held a Reserve commission, was waiting to be called, but to his great disappointment and disgust he was turned down because of nervous exhaustion from overwork.

It was Joseph's rejection that finally determined me. But again age reared its ugly head, and I too was turned down as a regular commissioned medical officer. But I was offered an alternative. I could go in as a contract surgeon with the "assimilated" rank of first lieutenant. That meant that while I would be wearing the regular Army officer's uniform, except that the caduceus insignia would have a C imposed on it to indicate the fact I was a contract surgeon, I would actually be a civilian employed by the Army in a kind of supplementary capacity. Since there was no way for me to turn the clock back seventeen years to the forty-five-year age limit prescribed by regulations, nor was there any way for me to get those regulations changed, I gladly accepted this second best. In due course, I was appointed to the Ninth Service Command, and in mid-March, 1943, I was ordered to Benicia Arsenal at Benicia, California, near San Francisco.

I immediately reported for duty and was cordially welcomed by Captain Howard H. Volan, who was in command of the arsenal's medical section. He promptly assigned me to the station hospital. It was not a very large installation, but was well equipped and staffed and operated with great efficiency. It was divided into two divisions, one that treated only military personnel, the other only civilian. Its one conspicuous lack was X-ray and laboratory facilities. In addition to the hospital, the arsenal also had two first-aid posts, a mobile medical unit and something called a "disaster train."

Although twenty-seven years had passed since my induction into the Italian Army's Medical Corps, my first days at Benicia reminded me forcibly of my Italian military experiences. The first similarity that hit me was the endless sea of paper we had to battle constantly. There were dozens of complicated forms that had to be filled out, and filled out in a precise "G.I." way. Then there were the countless reports that had to be written and, again, written in a precisely prescribed G.I. manner. Also—and this was something that plagued me and every physician during his first months of Army service—you had to write up your diagnosis, treatment and operations in an exact Army fashion. There was a mimeographed so-called "bible" which had been copied from the authorized list of diagnostic and therapeutic terms prepared in Washington, D. C., by the Surgeon General of the United States Army. These and only these were the terms we were permitted to employ in writing up a diagnosis or a treatment. For instance, we could not say that a soldier was suffering from a cold or even an upper respiratory infection, as we would in civilian practice. No, sir. We would have to enter on his chart or medical tag the diagnosis "Nasopharyngitis, acute," followed by the "degree of severity"—mild, moderate or severe. Or jaundice had to be officially set down as "Hepatitis." And so on and so on. The other doctors, who were all Army medical officers, constantly became angry at having to conform to this system; though I sometimes found it cumbersome, I was rather amused by the whole thing, realizing that all armies functioned in fundamentally the same manner.

In another respect I soon found the United States and Italian armies were similar. Both had their share of work-shirkers and loafers. But here I think the Italian method of dealing with "goldbricks" was more effective, not merely in getting the culprit back on the job but in keeping him there for good, or at least discouraging him from further gold-bricking. An Italian soldier who needlessly reported on sick call and who the medical officer suspected was faking received one of two "cures," neither very pleasant from the goldbrick's point of view: he either had an enormous dose of castor oil forced down his reluctant gullet, or he got a strong, hot enema; or in aggravated cases he would

get both. When I suggested introducing this form of therapy at
the arsenal, I was told that the United States Army preferred
to employ "psychology" in handling the goldbrick problem. I
strongly suspect that most troop commanders would have much
rather used my more drastic but far more practical methods.

A large part of our duties was giving physical examinations
to civilians applying for work in the arsenal. Although we
handled a rather large volume of examinations each day, they
occupied a surprisingly brief part of our time, because we were
required only to look for certain specified diseases or disabilities
which could later form the basis for a claim against the government if it could not be proved that it existed prior to the date
of the person's going to work for the government.

I remained at Benicia until the end of that summer. All
things considered, it was a happy period of my life. I felt I was
making my small contribution to the war effort: I was leading
a healthful, regular existence; I had formed many pleasant associations with the other doctors, nurses and several of the enlisted men; and my work, though quite strenuous at times, was
interesting and stimulating.

But all armies are the same in another respect: they never
let you remain long in one spot. When orders came in shipping
me to the Holding and Reconsignment Point at Pasco, Washington, I was anything but pleased. And I was even less pleased
when one of the arsenal officers told me he had been stationed
there himself and it was a "lousy hellhole," cold, windy, bleak,
close to the junction of the Columbia and Snake rivers. But
"orders is orders," and mine called for me to report at Pasco
within ten days. I promptly packed, got my travel orders and
headed north.

I arrived at Pasco shortly after midnight. My first glimpse
of the place certainly confirmed what I had been told about it.
The post consisted of a number of wooden cantonment-type
structures—they reminded me of the Austrian prison camps I
had been confined in—sprawled out on a flat, wide, barren plain.
It certainly appeared forlorn and desolate. Although it was only

August, the air was chill and biting. It was a much larger installation than the arsenal. There were some thirty-five officers, a complement of enlisted men and more than five hunderd full-time civilian employees. The civilians took care of receiving, storing and shipping the supplies that were stored in the enormous warehouses that constituted most of the Point's buildings.

The infirmary was a far more modern and better-equipped plant than Benicia's station hospital. I noticed, however, in the pharmacy that the supplies of penicillin and sulfa were still unopened, whereas such old standbys as castor oil, bicarbonate and aspirin were in great demand.

A week after I arrived my predecessor left and I took over and proceeded to get things organized. A few days later the colonel dropped in for a chat. He asked me what I thought of the infirmary. I told him I thought it was splendid, but wasn't it rather too large and elaborate for the post's needs? At that his face darkened and he said sharply, "Perhaps it may *seem* too large to you now, Doctor, but it won't if an epidemic should hit us. There's only one hospital in Pasco and it's quite small."

That was fine, I replied, but in the event of an epidemic a special isolation hospital would be required with specially assigned doctors, nurses and orderlies. It would be impossible to house infectious cases with regular hospital patients.

The colonel's face got blacker. I could see one of my nurses signaling me to keep quiet; but I have never been very adroit with the diplomatic lie, and in that instant, I saw no necessity for it. Even though I could see that the infirmary was the colonel's pet project, I had no intention of lying about it. I thought it was a waste of the taxpayers' money; and just because he had a "chicken" on his collar was no reason for me to have chicken in my heart. I am afraid that from then on the colonel and I were not exactly friends.

The fruits of my outspokenness soon ripened. The colonel went out of his way to make things as unpleasant as possible for me and to place as many obstacles in my way as he could. In his blind urge for imperial glory and splendor, he had gone ahead and constructed that magnificent infirmary, but he had forgot to reckon with the hard, sad facts of Army life. He had overlooked the prime one—the sacred "T/O & E," which is Armyese for "Table of Organization and Equipment." This could have been brought down from the heights of Sinai by Moses along with the Ten Commandments, for it was no less final and inflexible. Each and every unit in the entire Army had to follow a prescribed organizational scheme that had been set up in Washington. This set forth not only how many officers and enlisted men each unit was entitled to have, but precisely how many of each rank and for what duties. In addition, it specified exactly what equipment every unit, be it an infantry company, an ack-ack battery or a general hospital, was entitled to have and the quantity of each.

In building what was virtually a 250-bed station hospital for a post that did not warrant more than 50 or 75 beds, at most, the colonel had neglected to take into consideration the fact that the T/O would not make it possible to man it with a staff commensurately large. The result? As October started edging into November and the weather turned raw, cold and damp, activity picked up sharply in our infirmary. More and more people came down with severe colds, grippe, flu and other respiratory and chest ailments. Under ordinary circumstances, many of the less-acute cases would have "doctored" themselves at home. But with all the colonel's crowing about his grand hospital and his urging them to make use of its free facilities, they naturally came crowding into the infirmary.

I would not have objected to that in the least, had it not been for the fact we were sadly understaffed—a common, perennial complaint, I imagine, in all armies in all wars. The colonel had been hot for erecting a grandiose, showy structure (I feel sure that if he could have gotten away with it he would have named it after himself), but when it came to manning it adequately he had scrimped and stinted, using for other jobs the men the T/O specifically assigned to it. That was all right so long as we weren't busy, but once the flood started we were desperately short-handed.

Now was the moment the colonel chose to revenge himself on me. All my appeals for more men (all I asked for was the minimum staff prescribed by the T/O) were consistently turned down by post headquarters on the grounds that (1) no surplus manpower was available and (2) T/O & E prevents further expansion of the staff.

Of course, those who really suffered in consequence were the patients, who could not and did not get the service and care they should have received. There wasn't much the G.I.'s could do about it; but the civilian employees could do something about it and did, any number of them filing official complaints. And naturally, since I was ostensibly in charge of the infirmary, the blame was laid at my doorstep.

For a long time prior to this—in fact, it began a year or more before I entered the Army—I had been troubled by a gastrointestinal disturbance. I had dismissed it as nothing more than heartburn or gas or mild indigestion, since it was not very severe. But now, under the lash of this nerve-wracking situation, it started to kick up seriously. There were times when the pain was so sharp I came near to blacking out.

As it continued and the frequency of the attacks became greater I realized that I would have to do something about it. But I kept stalling, fearing that the cause was much graver than I wanted to believe. Finally, of course, I had to go to the McCaw General Hospital in Walla Walla for a checkup. There, my hunch was confirmed. I was suffering from gastroenterocolitis.

My medical officer proposed that I return to civilian life. I was violently against it. As long as the war was still going on I wanted to remain in uniform. Now that I knew what was bothering me, I would take care of it; after all, I was a doctor myself. But the captain pointed out that that was easy to say but difficult to do in the Army. As a physician, I knew that a carefully controlled diet is absolutely essential in the treatment of ulcer cases. How would I be able to control mine at some isolated post? Moreover, the constant stress and strain of military life wouldn't do my condition any good. "If you were your own patient, Doctor," he said to me, "you would give yourself the same prescription I'm giving you now: get out of the service."

All my arguments and appeals proved ineffective; he had made up his mind and quite frankly, I couldn't really blame him. The Army was no place for anyone with an ulcer. Indeed, I had myself recommended the discharge of several soldiers suffering from that ailment.

By the time all the paper work had been completed and reviewed and all the other formalities observed it was March, 1944, when I was "separated" from the United States Army. At that point, I might have attempted to resume my private practice. I had done my "bit" for my adopted country; I was sixty-five years old. No one could criticize me if I did not take any further direct part in the war effort. That is, no one except myself. For I knew I would be restless and quite unhappy if I wasn't doing *something,* no matter how small and unimportant, toward helping to defeat Germany and Japan.

Since the armed forces would not have anything to do with me, the next place was industry. I applied for a medical position with the California Shipbuilding Corporation at Terminal Island. Its medical department was headed by an eminent surgeon, Dr. Theodore I. Bluechel. He accepted me at once.

"Calship," as it was more popularly known, was the second-largest shipyard in the country. Its medical facilities were top-notch. There was a completely equipped modern hospital in the center of the yard with two first-aid stations situated at some distance to take care of immediate emergencies. And the staff, personally selected by Dr. Bluechel, was of the highest caliber.

During my first month at Calship I worked in the Male Department. Then one of the doctors in the Female Department left and I was assigned there. Most of my confreres shunned that assignment, but having had such a large percentage of

women patients during my practice, I did not in the least mind
treating them now.

Nevertheless, there was nothing easy about the job. As a
matter of fact, I worked much harder there than I ever had in
the Army. On an average, I examined and treated 125 women a
day; that breaks down to about fifteen-plus an hour. Of course,
on such a basis, it wasn't possible to give them as much attention
as one would have liked to give them. But it was possible to give
them more than merely adequate care, and those who required
more extensive study and therapy I would refer to hospitals or
outside specialists. The largest portion of the cases I handled
involved occupational accidents, fractures, bruises, cuts and third-
degree burns. Occupational diseases also formed a large part of
my "practice" there—fatigue, nervous exhaustion and various
debilitative diseases such as shingles, insomnia and anemia.

The women defense workers could be divided into two
distinct groups, I found. One consisted of those who, after a
hard day's labor, went home and put in a hard night's labor
of housework, fixing dinner for their husbands and families,
looking after their children, cleaning the house and taking care
of all the other innumerable household chores that had piled
up during the course of the day. The other group consisted of
playgirls, many of whom were also wives and mothers. They
would rush home from work, change into fancy clothes and go
out all night dancing, drinking and who knows what else? Very
often they would just have time to go home, change back into
work clothes and report at the plant. Both groups, however, presented serious medical problems, since neither followed a living
pattern that was exactly conducive to good health.

I sweated out the end of the war at Calship and did not quit
there until September, 1945. Then I found myself faced with
the same problem that was facing millions upon millions of
young Americans—readjustment. How was I to get back to
civilian life? What was I going to do now?

Most of my fellow war workers talked over the situation with
their fathers. I talked mine over with my sons. They felt that I

had more than earned the right to follow Whitman's counsel and "loaf and invite my soul" and watch the world go by. I had been able to put by enough to provide for my few simple needs; and if it should not prove sufficient, they were both doing well in the practice of medicine and would gladly furnish me with anything I might ever require.

21 : Final Diagnosis

THERE ALWAYS COMES that moment in the treatment of any case when the physician is ready to discharge his patient and must sum up the result of all his findings in what is known as "the final diagnosis." It may not necessarily be the correct one; the physician may have been in error about the case right from the beginning. But according to his own best judgment, for better or for worse, this summation represents his last word on the subject.

What has my life added up to? What have I accomplished? Well, the answers are far from easy. What, actually, does any man's life mean? A certain amount of happiness and joy, a certain amount of sorrow, grief, disappointment and tragedy. It adds up to moments of love and ecstasy, to moments of dark despair, loneliness, hatred. It adds up to accomplishment and to frustration, to success and to failure. For one the percentage of fulfillment and happiness will assay higher than for another. What causes that, I have no idea. Whether the fault be in our stars or in ourselves, I do not know—though I strongly suspect it generally lies in ourselves.

In my own case, I would be rather at a loss if I were compelled to decide whether my three quarters of a century added up to success or failure, to happiness or sorrow. Judged simply and solely by the worldly measure of things, mine I am afraid could not be called a "success story." I have not accumulated great wealth; in fact, I have never earned at any time in my existence anything that might be called "big money." I have not achieved fame. There are no medical institutions that bear my name. There are no great medical discoveries associated with me. I have not gained any position of power and importance in public affairs. Thus from a purely mundane standpoint my life has been anything but a resounding, resplendent triumph.

Yet in spite of that, as I now survey my own lifework I must confess to a sense of deep satisfaction. No, I am not being smug and complacent, nor am I indulging in self-justification. At least I do not think I am. We are all familiar with the Abbé Sièyes' famous answer when he was asked what he had done during the French Revolution: "I lived through it." So, perhaps, I might make the same response; I too have lived through seventy-five years of wars, depressions, disasters, changes, upheavals, crises, disappointments, triumphs. There are those who might reckon this, in and of itself, as a definite accomplishment.

But more than that, I think, are some solid, definite items that can be entered on the "plus" side of the great ledger of life. I think I have served society usefully and have at least pulled my own weight in the boat. If I have not won a brilliant reputation as a man of medicine, I have certainly done my share to help keep mankind healthy and happy, content to perform my task in obscurity.

Then, I can say I have spent seventy-five years on this earth without doing any injury, knowingly or willingly, to any fellow human being.

More than that, however, I can claim having won and earned and kept the love, devotion and faith of one of the most wonderful women the Lord ever created. How many people can say, truthfully, that they have fully and truly possessed and been possessed by another in this sense?

And finally I feel that I can take pride and real satisfaction from what I conceive to be my finest, greatest contribution to the world—my two sons. Both have done credit not alone to me but to the community which has made an investment in them as it has in every one of its members. Joseph, denied the privilege of serving his country in its wartime struggle, has become a fine doctor with an excellent practice in Los Angeles. Italo, after thirty months of wartime service in the Pacific and several decorations, elected to remain in the Army and is today a lieutenant colonel in the Medical Corps and is stationed in Virginia.

It is also customary, as a rule, for a doctor in writing up his final diagnosis to offer the patient some prognosis, some forecast of the future. Will he suffer from his disease any further? Or will it improve? Or will it develop possible complications? In my own case, I fear the prognosis must be quite sketchy and vague—so sketchy and so vague, in fact, as to be virtually non-existent. After all, I have exceeded my allotted biblical span by five years. What more of the future can I claim? Or want? The truth of the matter is that I shall be quite content to be able to say about the years to come what I have been able to say about those that are past: *I lived through them.*